PRAY
GIVE
GO
DO

[Extreme faith in an awesome God]

PRAY GIVE GO DO

[Extreme faith in an awesome God]

Dave Barker
with Lee Jordan

MONARCH
BOOKS

Mill Hill, London & Grand Rapids, Michigan

Copyright © Dave Barker and Lee Jordan 2003.
The right of Dave Barker and Lee Jordan to be identified
as authors of this work has been asserted by them in
accordance with the Copyright, Designs
and Patents Act 1988.

Published by Monarch Books in the UK 2003,
Concorde House, Grenville Place,
Mill Hill, London NW7 3SA.

Text illustrations by Doreen Lang

Distributed by:
UK: STL, PO Box 300, Kingstown Broadway, Carlisle,
Cumbria CA3 0QS.

ISBN 1 85424 589 9 (UK)
ISBN 0 8254 6221 5 (USA)

British Library Cataloguing Data
A catalogue record for this book is available from the
British Library.

Designed and produced for the publishers by
Gazelle Creative Productions, Mill Hill, London NW7 3SA.

Printed and bound in Great Britain by Bookmarque Ltd, Croydon

CONTENTS

ACKNOWLEDGEMENTS

My special thanks to:

**Sue Knight – for collating my
words and thoughts**
Katie Jenson – for the original layout
Lee Jordan – for putting it all together
**Ruth Box, Tessa Haynes, Sharon Francis,
Stephen Montgomery, Daniel Leakey,
Stephanie Burrows, Marco Palmer, John Piper,
Emma Ridgewell, Lisa Burgess – for their
various articles (*What4* team members)**

Jane Holloway – for her article (Evangelical Alliance)
Bernard Terlouw – for his article (MAF – Kenya)
Tony Campolo – for his foreword and article

Dave Barker, June 2003

Dave Barker is the director of the Christian youth organization *What4*, as well as a youth pastor, church leader and conference speaker. He has preached to politicians in the corridors of power at Westminster and high-profile events such as Spring Harvest and Cross Rhythms. The *What4* ministry is dedicated to motivating and mobilizing thousands of young people for mission and enabling them to go out into the world with the Gospel message. His desire is to see youth making a stand for Jesus, and showing their peers that the Christian life is radical and life-changing, and that young people can make a difference if God is for them. Dave Barker burns with a desire to communicate Jesus to our hurting planet. Dave's prayer is that this book helps the fire to spread.

Lee Jordan is a writer and freelance journalist: he has been an active team member of Cheriton Baptist's youth group where Dave is the Youth Pastor. Lee has helped to put Dave's passion for God into words.

We want you to know

What4 is involved in many projects in the UK, Europe and overseas, especially in Africa and Asia. Many of the accounts which you will read in this book feature people from those vast continents but *What4* would like readers to know that mission begins where you are, right now! You can focus globally but apply yourself locally! It is the *What4* team's prayer that we will be on the front line as the youth of Christ go out into all the countries on earth and proclaim the Gospel in word and by practical application. No doubt their stories will be told in a future book as these young 21st-century disciples take the world for Christ. Though the war is won, many battles remain. But with Jesus as our Lord, victory is assured!

🌀 Foreword

The mission of the Church is missions. Jesus called us to go into all the world and preach the Gospel. He himself was a missionary. He was sent from God to declare the Kingdom of God here on earth. Those of us who claim to be his followers must also be missionaries in one way or another. We must pray, give, go and do – and that is what this book is all about.

Missionary work is not just church planting. It is the declaration that the Kingdom of God is at hand. Jesus came declaring the kingdom. Each of the Synoptic Gospels begins with a declaration that Jesus proclaimed that the Kingdom of God was available to all of us and that we should repent and prepare for it. When he taught his disciples to pray, in what has come to be called The Lord's Prayer, he told us to pray for the kingdom. His parables were about the Kingdom of God. One of the last things he said to his disciples before ascending into Heaven, following his resurrection, were things concerning the kingdom.

There are many descriptions of the Kingdom of God in Scriptures, but I choose to focus on the passage that we find in Isaiah, chapter 65:17 and the verses that follow. There, the Kingdom of God is declared to be a new society in which people have decent houses to live in, and where there is good employment so that every man and woman is paid a just salary. The kingdom is to be a place where children do not die in infancy, and when children are born, mothers do not have to worry if their children will be blown away in a gang war, destroyed by drugs, or other such painful calamities that are all too evident among young people in our world today.

We further find that the Kingdom of God is a place where old people live out their lives in fullness of health and where people do not "hurt the earth anymore". That last phrase means people will be environmentally conscious. They will protect the earth from the kind of polluting that has been common in our urban industrial society. The Kingdom of God is where God's will is done on earth as it is in Heaven. It is a society in which all social institutions are ruled by justice and in which there is health and well-being for all citizens. This is the world we are supposed to create. In Romans, chapter 8 we are told that all of creation is groaning and waiting for the sons and the daughters of God to rise up and to join with God in the creating of this world.

I have no illusions about our ability to create the perfect society, but I do know that the Christ we believe in is coming back again. As it says in Philippians chapter 1:6, "He who began a good work in you will carry it on to completion until the day of Christ Jesus." That means God is at work among us and is with us in building the kingdom, and as we commit ourselves to this great enterprise, we find the meaning for our lives and the purpose of our being.

This mission is not an option for Christians. It is our very reason to exist. When Christ saved us he did not save us for the next world, but for this world. He wanted us to be open to the infilling of his spirit, so that through us he could work for justice, feed the poor, deliver the oppressed and help to restructure the society in which we live into the kind of world that God wants it to be.

To this end, missionaries have been entering every sector of society to be agents of change. They see the political world waiting to be invaded by those with biblical visions of justice. They look at the economic structures of society and commit themselves to economic development that will bring well-being to those who are now hungry and have been marginalized because of poverty. They look at the educational system and see it as a realm that is open to those who want to touch the lives of children and mould a future generation into people of God. They see the Church as the Body of Christ that could be his hands doing the work that needs to be done in this world.

Dave Barker has a deep commitment to youth. He knows better than most that young people need a commitment in order to develop identity. "Self" that is not something that is gained through introspection, regardless of what the pop psychologists of our times might say. It only comes when young people find a cause that is worthy of their humanity. Victor Frankl, the founder of Logo Therapy, said so well in his book *Man's Quest for Meaning* that it is only by envisioning a noble purpose for life that one has the capacity to escape the neurotic tendencies that are in all of us. It is purpose and meaning that delivers us from the insanity of the inane. It is having something worth dying for that gives to each of us something worth living for. This is especially true for the young people for whom this book is primarily written.

If we lose this generation of young people from the Church, it will not be because we have demanded too much of them, but because we have demanded too little. Instead of holding up a Jesus who, in the words of Dietrich Bonhoeffer, bids us "come and die", we have offered a Jesus who simply endorses the superficial lifestyle prescribed for young people by the media that expects little in the way of sacrifice. We have created what Kenneth Kenniston, the social commentator, has called "the generation of the uncommitted". Identity comes to a young person when that individual defines what is ultimate and eternal and is ready to give his or her life for the calling that ultimacy requires.

Identity comes to anyone who is ready to take up the cross and heed the call of Jesus. That is what mission is all about. It is as we are heeding the Great Commission given to us by God in Christ that we begin to define who we are. In sociology the process is called "praxis". Contrary to those who think that we discover who we are before we act, the concept of praxis postulates that it is only in the context of action that we experience self-discovery. That is why I say when young people heed the call to the mission of God, and act on that call, they will begin to discover the meanings of their lives and the purposes for which they have been created.

While the mission of the Church can be carried out in every sector of the world that constitutes everyday life, there is a special need for every one of us to consider spending some time away from those settings with which we are familiar and in which we have become comfortable. It is only by stepping outside of the world in which we live that we are able to gain a perspective on it and see it in both its potentialities and in its shortcomings. That is why I have always insisted that my university students travel to third world countries and spend time among the poor and the oppressed, working and ministering as best as they can. While they do a lot of good for the people they go to serve, what is most notable is that the Christians who participate in these short-term mission programmes (whether they be for a week, a month, a year or even more), experience a second conversion. They go through a consciousness change and come back to their own world with new insights. They almost feel like aliens in a strange and distant land when they return to their hometown communities. They see the wastefulness of our affluent lifestyle and the meaninglessness of the socially prescribed careerism that hitherto permeated their consciousness. Short-term excursions into the third world break the hold that the dominant culture in which they were raised has had on them. They realize that not only do those in the third world need help, but those who have been lulled into the comfortable, attractive, tasteful, relaxed and unconscious form of middle class affluent slavery also need salvation. I find that most young people have to go away in order to come back and see the world in which they live as it really is, and in that returning, experience the challenge to change their world into the kind of world God wants it to be.

If young people are to go, they must be sent. Those of us who long for them to be people of vision must be ready to finance their excursions into the worlds of poverty that await them in distant lands. We must be ready to pray for them that the Holy Spirit will deliver them from simply being religious pietists, and enable them to encounter the Jesus who saved them, as they look into the eyes of the oppressed. We must pray that they will not look down on those whom they go to serve, but will be humbled by them and made to see their own poverty of spirit, and thus be driven to repentance and renewal.

The mission of the Church is indeed missions. And as the people of the Church become involved in missions away from home they will learn what is necessary to be a missionary in those places they call home. Thus mission requires our all as Christians. Our lives must be organized around his calling.

Tony Campolo, Ph.D.
Professor of Sociology
Eastern University, USA

🌀 Introduction

I have been involved in the youth ministry for over 21 years and have had the incredible privilege of telling thousands of young people the Gospel message and seeing them make radical stands as they choose to give their lives to God. The believer's walk isn't easy: Jesus didn't say that it would be. It means the total commitment of our lives. When I consider what it means to be a Christian – a dedicated follower of Jesus Christ – I believe, passionately, that four foundational areas are at the very heart of effective discipleship. To be a true disciple of Jesus in the 21st century, his people are going to have to pray, give, go and do. Now, it doesn't take a lot of brain power to understand these four principles, or realizing this is what Christians are called to do on a daily basis, but implementing them is another matter.

Pray Give Go Do

The Christian life is supposed to be challenging, but don't worry, we are not alone. As you read through this book you will hear personal stories of young people who are running the "spiritual" gauntlet, and who by practically applying these four precepts (above) to their faith have won battles for Jesus' coming kingdom. God will reward his workers. By praying, giving, going and doing these young people have witnessed and experienced the life-changing effects that God desires to bring about in all of us: whether young or old, male or female.

⦿ Did you know?

The Bible has been the most read book – ever! The most controversial, the first mass-produced, with more copies printed than any other book in history.

Throughout the experiences that I have gained as a youth pastor, church leader, school teacher and as national director of the Christian youth organisation *What4*, I am never more satisfied than when I see young people grasp what it is to have a relationship with God. I am overwhelmed as they talk to God through prayer; encouraged when they understand the value of giving to God (this can mean their time, money, energy and any other area of their lives that they want to surrender to the one that made them); inspired when they realize that their school and home is their mission field and this is where they have to share Jesus with their friends and classmates. These young Christians are leading by example because they understand it is vital to pray, give, go and do. They know that Jesus, God in the skin, becomes the centre of everything; whether in church, at the meal table, watching TV, listening to music, going for a swim – whatever the pursuit, they pursue God first.

There's nothing in the Bible, God's very own Word, that says his people can't have fun. What he asks in return is for us to be in line with his thinking. He knows best. God will never disappoint us when we honour him in this way. So take comfort from this fact: he wants us to communicate and he wants it to be a two-way conversation. Forget BT and your mobile, try GT instead – God talk!

To be encouraged, a warrior needs their sword

Let's face it. We will never get very far in our relationships with God and people unless we offer encouragement to others. This works both ways: we have to receive encouragement, otherwise we will suffer burnout. Just envisage a famous footballer giving the fans their goals, but not being cheered on when he scores. Or turn the situation around and think how the supporters will feel if they are urging their players on but their team doesn't care. We all need to be encouraged.

A great biblical example of what I am talking about is a man called Joshua. He is one of the

Bible's great warriors of God. In Joshua chapter 1:8–9, we read of God's encouragement to Joshua. God commands him not to fear, not to be discouraged, as the Lord will be with him wherever he goes. Just imagine the responsibility that Joshua had. He had been chosen as Moses' successor to lead the Israelites into the Promised Land. He was on the verge of crossing over the River Jordan with all his people trusting him. Not only that, he was following in the great Moses' footsteps. What an awesome challenge. What if that was you? Think of all those questions you would be dying to ask: Why me? How can I be good enough? I'm too thick, aren't I? What if I fail? Joshua needed to know that God would be with him, that he would not be abandoned. It was a massive task to complete, but fearful as he was, he decided to put his trust in God.

Likewise in this gadget-obsessed new millennium where the material has suffocated the spiritual, we are called to follow God as his disciples and not to fear others or the awkward, dodgy and sometimes perilous situations that we might and probably will find ourselves in. God spoke to Joshua about the importance of knowing the book of the Law (the Bible before Jesus came), not letting it depart from his mouth, meditating on it day and night, so that he might be careful to do everything written in it; then he would prosper and be successful.

HAVEN'T YOU HEARD?
GOD TALKS TO YOU WHEN YOU
STUDY HIS WORD.

You are just as important as Joshua is!

Okay, you might not have to lead your entire country through the wilderness but your challenge is just as big because it is relational to you and your circumstances. God is with you just like he was with Joshua. So the rules that applied to him apply to you too. We need to know his book, the Bible – it's our map for life. His Word will show us how to pray, to give, to go and to do.

You may not become prosperous and successful as the world defines these two concepts: meaning material possessions like money, houses, designer clothes and fast cars, but you will achieve success in the way that God wants it – and that is the only way that matters. God knows best.

The Bible says: *"If God is for us, who can be against us?"* (Romans 8:31). Yes, there will be obstacles confronting you, some bigger than others, but they will fall. There will be tears of sadness, but also tears of joy, times of thirst and hunger, but also times of quenching and filling. Whatever the world and its followers throw at you, always remember that Jesus is a breath away and soon the people of the world are going to fall on their knees – some in shame, some in adoration – because one day he is returning to planet earth. And if anyone suffers for Jesus, whether it is because of bullying or mocking, or rejection, or in any other way, then grab hold tightly of the fact that God knows what you have done for him and he will not forget. His rewards you will keep forever! So as you read on, my heart's desire is that you will be inspired and motivated to pray, give, go and do.

Dave Barker
National Director, *What4*

🌀 Chapter 1

Pray

Q What For?

A *To seek your Destiny*

⠿ To get you thinking

Dr Donald Coggan, a former Archbishop of Canterbury, was once asked: "Aren't answers to your prayers just coincidences?"

"No," he replied. "The difference is that when I pray, the coincidences happen, and when I don't pray they don't!"

From God to you (Don't look a gift horse in the mouth)

Most people would say that they have prayed at some time in their lives. The majority pray when they are in trouble and do not know what to do, when natural resources are exhausted. This goes for many Christians too!

We must ask ourselves: do we really know what prayer is all about? I'm going to be bold and suggest that there are three types of praying people. Firstly there is the prayer warrior. This person really believes in the power of prayer and is not afraid to talk with God about all sorts of things. This warrior really takes authority in the fact that he or she is a child of God and has no doubts that Jesus is seated on his throne in Heaven. The warrior truly expects God to answer all requests. He or she will pray until the door is opened and will not take "no" for an answer (see Luke 11:5–10).

The next person only prays about selfish things that will benefit them and does not very often consider the needs of others. Perhaps the prayer of "self" is an apt description.

The third person never thinks of prayer unless their circumstances are desperate and, even then, their joined hands and creaking knees represent that all options have been tried and prayer is the last resort – whether they believe that there is a God in Heaven doesn't really matter. This is more like a pleading to hope, rather than a heartfelt cry to the Creator of the universe – the one who holds life in his hand.

A true Christian should be praying beyond the concept of hope. In secular (people of the world) terms, hope is a chance that the dice of fate rolls in your favour. But for a disciple of Jesus, hope is the assurance and certainty that God's plan for you will never fail (take a look at just one of God's promises in Romans 8:28).

Before you read on, take a deep breath

In case you have forgotten, please breathe… NOW!

You are still not ready yet to contemplate the one who made you. Close your eyes and thank God for who he is before you continue. Now take a hold of these facts. As Christians pray we have the awesome privilege of communicating with the God who placed the stars in the sky and named every one of them! Through prayer we liaise with the one who created time, even though he exists outside of time, yet still controls it!

If your brain is beginning to ache, wait one moment, there's more… God, your heavenly Father knew you before you were born (Ephesians 1:4) and he is the one that knit you together in your mother's womb and knows all your thoughts before you even think them, and he allotted you the days you have and will live; they are recorded in his book! Sounds too good to be true? You want proof? Then check out Psalm 139.

After you read this amazing poetic song to God, because that's what a psalm is, you'll think wow! This God is worth taking a closer look at.

You see, God will never ask you to do

anything that you cannot do. He is already planning for you. You might think, no way, not me. But God already knows your future and has promised to be with you through the good times and the bad. When God came to earth in the person of Jesus, to walk among the human race, to rescue people from their wrongdoings – sins – he did it so that we could have a relationship with him. Jesus was a man but at the same time he was and is and will always be the Son of God and the Son of Man. When Jesus began his rescue mission 2,000 years ago by coming to our world he gave up paradise in Heaven to be like one of us, but this is the brain twister – he was 100 per cent fully human but at the same time 100 per cent fully God! Don't try and fathom it, it's a massive thought. Some answers we will have to wait for. When we get to Heaven we will be able to ask him – personally! But for now, let's get on with what he wants us to do on planet earth.

By praying and reading our Bibles we'll start to know what God's plan for our own lives is. What better way than to model our individual prayer life on Jesus' meditations with God.

Remember he is not expecting us to do anything he hasn't already done. Wow, what a rich inheritance we have.

When we read the Gospels of Matthew, Mark, Luke and John, we learn about the incredible life of Jesus and how vital prayer was to him. A disciple by definition is someone who follows another; surely we should do what Jesus did. After all, he is God's own Son. (See John 5:19–30.) Jesus has to be our paragon of prayer. From him we learn how to pray, whom we pray to and what we pray for.

In the Bible there are many references on the subject of prayer, because there is so much that God wants us to learn from him and communicate to the world. Prayer is our most powerful weapon and it just like God to want to help us. When he says pray, the Holy Spirit will be searching our hearts – clearing out the rubbish and guiding our words and thoughts. And not just when we are in trouble but every time we seek God in prayer. It's a two-way deal!

Jesus never asked his followers to kiss their brains away. The disciple's walk has to be practical as well as relying on the supernatural. If you are anything like me, I think it is great, where possible, to go and see the place you are going to pray for; to experience a venue, even to become accustomed to the smells as you walk around the location as you prepare to pray; whether it be a building, a street, a city, wherever and whatever it is, it's good to get to know your surroundings first.

Of course, this isn't always feasible or necessary for successful praying. You can pray anywhere. It might be in your own room, where you can be more intimate because no one else is around to bother you. Jesus took himself off to be alone and talk to his Father (Mark 1:35). In the quiet and stillness of your private place, open-heart prayers are easier.

But you might find God wants you to pray in a public place. Now not many people are comfortable with the thought of falling on to their knees in a busy building or high-street shop when masses of people are close by, especially when many of them think being so open about your faith is "weird" and they might consider you as one of those "Jesus Freaks".

Anyway, kneeling in a bustling environment is inviting trouble; someone might fall over you! So, again, we have to be practical and respect other people: the right Bible-based attitude is essential. But if you mingle with the crowd, who's to know what you are doing? As long as God does, then so what? Besides, if God wants you to make a spectacle of yourself and you are willing, then he will give you the strength and peace of mind to accomplish it.

The surroundings are not important, where you are will not make your prayers any more effective – whether in a silent, peaceful place or a noisy, hectic venue, genuine prayers are always powerful. One way is not better than the other is,

though a quiet location does help you to think and it's easier to seek God's peace when your ears are not being bombarded with noise. But at the end of the day it's all about doing what God is asking you to do, and that is to stay in line with his will. If you are not sure what his will is for a certain situation then pray to him and read his Word – you are guaranteed to find out what he wants you to do.

Lots of people say, "Well, if God spoke to me and let me ask him questions then I might believe in him and start doing what he wants me to do." Such people can't see the wood for the trees. They just don't realize that he has spoken to the human race – what he said is in the Bible, and God is as good as his Word; you can stand by it. And God's not finished! He speaks through his believers – the Church – and he uses all kinds of people.

You can talk to him, this is what prayer is all about, and he will answer you. But how do you know it's him and not your own imagination? God may not answer you audibly, but he will work through your circumstances and if you are listening, then you will hear! And if you need it repeating, then keep on praying and reading your Bible – his Word never changes, you can rely on it 100 per cent. God chooses to bypass mobile phones and e-mails; he doesn't need them, he has access to your heart and soul. You can talk to him… anywhere!

On a personal note, I am not good at sitting still, and so, whether I am praying in London, in a foreign country, on the street, in schools or taking the dog for a walk, being on the move helps me when I am chatting to God.

Over a number of years I have travelled with loads of young people – just like you – on buses, in cars, in minibuses, from the south coast up to London for all-night prayer sessions. Together we walk around the streets of Soho, pray for the homeless on the Embankment, go into the House of Commons and pray with MPs, and pray outside Buckingham Palace and Number 10 Downing Street.

These have been tremendous times of encouragement as we have prayed for our nation and the countries of the world. Hundreds of young people have been touched with a fresh passion to pray, as they have put sightseeing to one side, and chosen to prayer-walk and to pray for all types of people. The capital city of any nation houses the whole spectrum of human beings, including colours, religions, personalities and cultures.

You too can join these amazing prayer times. (Take a look at our prayer projects that will tell you how you can become involved – see the Appendix at the end of the book.)

JOIN THIS NEW GENERATION THAT IS RISING TO PRAY LOCALLY AND GLOBALLY

Prayer is a powerful weapon

The above heading is true but as with all weapons there has to be a target, you have to take aim and, at the right moment, fire. These same principles can be applied to prayer. Prayer is our

Powersurge!

In December each year, **What4** organizes a mega nationwide prayer event in the capitals of Great Britain – London, Edinburgh, Cardiff and Belfast – to pray for the people who live and work in these cities, our nation and for the world. Powersurge also allows groups of young people to meet MPs in order to pray about the strategical areas of these cities – where there are poverty, the homeless, violence, gangs, trouble and spiritual darkness.

Each Powersurge centre is linked throughout the night via the mobile phone network, where requests for prayer and updates can be shared.

Powersurge takes place in June, on midsummer's night. It is another opportunity for thousands of young people to link up in prayer with Christians around the world.

communication line, without it we might as well speak to a tree. Fine if that's what you want to do but you won't get any answers. You want to try branching out!

God is not in nature. He created nature! So trees belong to him, as do all created things, including you and me.

Don't be ashamed to talk to God

Donna is a teenager and a member of a

youth group. She is a person who has had more than her fair share of difficulties and hassles. But she is not the type to seek sympathy and does not wallow in self-pity. She suffers from a growth problem and it was while Donna was having major surgery on her back that her prayer life, which was strong before the operations commenced, helped a number of young Christians to focus and get serious about their own prayer lives.

I can remember visiting her in hospital with a bunch of her young Christian mates. When I saw her I felt choked because she was in a lot of pain and we were wondering whether or not we should pray. I really wanted to but I felt embarrassed because of the nurses and doctors, and the general hive of activity that a hospital ward represents.

There was I, a youth pastor who had spoken in front of thousands of people about prayer and God, yet when it came down to it I felt like bottling it.

The group explained to Donna that we all felt really shy and uncomfortable but that we would pray for her... quietly! Donna may have been suffering, but in her own direct but gentle way she responded with words that I'll never forget:

"Don't be embarrassed, I have been going around praying for the patients in this ward. I have been praying for you and if you cannot pray for me, I would love to pray for you where you are right now. Oh yes, and I will be praying out loud, too!"

That was a defining moment and one of those precious times because without exception all of us prayed for Donna, and then in turn for one another. It was a brilliant prayer moment. The presence of God was in that ward and surrounded Donna's bed. God used Donna to encourage us to pray right where we were. Donna was not prepared to take "no" for an answer; for that matter nor is God. If we are open to him, he will meet with us. Donna showed by faith and obedience that she was open. We need to follow her example when we are in situations that only God through prayer can resolve.

Be proud to be a Jesus Freak

On another occasion I was meeting with my

mate Clive and a few other people. When we plan a big event we always say, "Hey, let's just pray about it, just commit it to God."

At this particular time the venue for prayer was Clacket Lane, one of the M25 service stations, where people go to have something to eat, or shop, or use the toilet facilities. We just prayed a simple prayer, certainly in faith, because the event was not going to happen if God didn't want it to. Thirty minutes later we stopped praying, and I guess we had been too loud, because when we looked up, it was like an exodus had taken place: the restaurant was deserted and we felt like Jesus Freaks, for all the wrong reasons, or so we thought.

The people must have felt uncomfortable and could not have been too sure what these "nutters" had been doing. As we were about to leave, one of the waiters, who was hovering around, approached Clive and me. He said, "You guys must be Christians."

It struck me at that moment that our prayers can also be a positive witness to others. Some people run away, but others take note and hopefully begin a relationship with God. In the Bible Jesus teaches that the world and its people will know who is a Christian: "By their fruit you will recognize them" (Matthew 7:16–20). So how we live and pray will identify to the sceptical world the true disciples of Jesus.

Just pause to think about your own prayer life. Does it reveal to others that you are a Christian?

God wants you to talk to him; he desires a

two-way conversation, whatever you are doing and wherever you are and however you feel. It doesn't matter if you are partying, if you are happy or depressed, he wants to talk with you.

The Bible and prayer are two channels that God has chosen to operate through. He promises to always be with his followers. That means you and me. He never changes. What he said thousands of years ago was sealed in the pages of his holy Word: "Ask and it will be given to you; seek and you will find… " (Matthew 7:7–12). And you can start right now! What are you waiting for?

What kind of prayers do you pray?

Don't forget that wherever you go Jesus wants to talk with you. Want proof? Well, read on.

A few years ago, some members of *What4*

◩ Copy Jesus

In John 17 we see how Jesus prayed for himself. This really shows us that though Jesus was God in the flesh he was also totally human as well. He was doing what he asks us to do. If it's good enough for Jesus then dare we <u>not</u> do as he did? He knew without prayer his mission would not succeed – nor will ours.

Jesus prayed for himself, for those close to him and we see him praying for all believers. What a perfect model Jesus has left for us to copy. So we should be praying for the people we work with, our classmates, other believers – our churches and their youth groups all around the world, Christian Unions, family and friends. This is the amazing privilege that God – the one who made everything – has given you and me. We simply have to do it. God says, "His will be done", so we'd better get praying. Awesome things happen when we honour God in this way: God is made known to a hurting and confused world, people are blessed, and the faithful ones who pray will receive incredible rewards in Heaven. Take hold of the awe-inspiring responsibility that you have as a believer in Christ.

🐾 Royal prayers

The King of the universe is praying for you, right now! He is seated at the right hand of God the Father. His mission is ongoing; it didn't end when he ascended to Heaven. He is preparing a place in paradise for all those who put their trust in him. For this is where they will be spending eternity. It doesn't stop there. He is interceding (pleading our cause to his Father), he is praying for YOU. Take another deep breath before you read on!

Right, breathe out and now read an awesome fact – your prayers join with Jesus' prayers!

were on a twelve-mile trek from one village in Ethiopia to another, where we were delivering urgent medical supplies. Our team consisted of eight people. As we set off we were full of faith and expectancy, excited as we committed the journey to the Lord. A local guide, who only knew one English word – "yes" – accompanied us. When any of us did attempt to ask him about directions he would just respond with a positive, "yes". We trusted in him as he had travelled the route many times.

The trek took longer than anticipated and we were warned to keep to the trail and not to wander off, and definitely not to wade through the river that ran its course close by – it was full of crocodiles! Another disconcerting warning was not to walk after dark, because this was when "unhelpful people" lurked nearby and would mug and loot anyone they came across.

Eleven hours into the journey we came across a giant convergence of two rivers. A major problem confronted the team. The footbridge that took travellers safely over it had been washed away. We were in a dilemma. Should we turn back? This caused anxiety: without the medical supplies that we were carrying, people would suffer. Another problem to compound the situation was the fact that our water provision was running low. The day was intensely hot and we were down to a few drops!

Of course, worry crept in. But we did not hesitate to pray to God that he would give wisdom to our guide, and that he would know what to do. So when the guide proceeded in his confident manner towards the river, we quickly followed. I wondered if I was witnessing a miracle – it looked like we were walking on water! Our trusty guide was leading us through a raised, seemingly invisible, pathway across the rivers.

Dusk was falling and the team, suffering from blisters, was growing tired. And we were nervous. It was like a scene from an Indiana Jones film when we virtually surfed down an eroding, dried-up waterfall. When we finally landed safely we found ourselves in long wild grass – its stems were mammoth size and grew above our heads. Panic set in. I was engulfed with apprehension; dusk had turned to night.

An African night is dense; out in the wilderness there are no flashing, Western lights or fluorescent advertising boards. The night-time that we were experiencing was pitch black, and the only sounds were coming from the surrounding wildlife.

Unbeknown to each one of us, we had all started to pray the same prayer, which translated to: "God, help us through this nightmare!" Boy, did God move fast: within ten minutes a tall, half-naked, muscle-bulging man appeared who looked like some mythical god. He was carrying a lethal AK38 machine-gun.

To say he looked mean would have been a pathetic understatement. We all feared the same thing – was this one of the "unhelpful people" we had been warned to avoid? But the size of an apparent enemy is no obstacle to the all-knowing God and he had heard our prayers. As fear started to course through each member of the team, God was already acting to bring about a safe conclusion to our unknown future.

Suddenly, eight young people emerged from the darkness and approached us; they all spoke excellent English and explained that they lived in the village that we were journeying to. The Ethiopian "god" lookalike was their armed guard.

Their first question immediately dispelled any fear. "Would you like us to help you by carrying your bags?" They also bore gifts of bananas and water. We were so thankful. They then proceeded to lead us through a secret short cut to their village.

Paul says in Hebrews 11:1 "Now faith is being sure of what we hope for and certain of what we do not see." I can personally declare this statement is true. We later discovered that our young rescuers had been travelling for a whole day from a market miles away; in fact in the opposite direction to their village. Yet they felt compelled to head home. Two of the young people were Christians and when we relayed to them our story they realized that God was drawing them back home to help their foreign brothers and sisters in Christ.

We were people they had never met before, but that didn't matter because when you trust in Jesus you become a member of the greatest family ever. Isn't it exciting that God has already gone before us: he is omniscient (all-knowing), omnipotent (all-powerful) and omnipresent (he is everywhere). God is not constrained to the dimensions of time. He is spirit and beyond our comprehension; yet because he sent his Son, Jesus, who is God in the flesh, we have someone who walked on earth and experienced what it is to be human with all the problems that are ours in a sinful world. He knows what we are going through. He even suffered torture and death on a cross so he could save us and show us a better way that will last forever. To receive the riches he wants to give to us, we Christians have to trust in God. That is what praying is all about – you can trust him!

DOES GOD ANSWER PRAYER OR WHAT!

Elijah was flesh and blood just like you and me!

There are so many prayer warriors in the Bible – Elijah is a man who knew how to pray. Check him out and see how he sought God's guidance through prayer.

James (the New Testament writer) in his letter to the churches used Elijah as a prayer model, and when you think that the Holy Spirit was working through James, it means that God was giving his personal seal of approval to Elijah's prayer life. Just take a look at James 5:16–18: "The prayer of a righteous man is powerful and effective. Elijah was a man just like us. He prayed earnestly that it would not rain, and it did not rain on the land for three and a half years. Again he prayed, and the heavens gave rain, and the earth produced its crops." James here is recounting Elijah's dedication to prayer. You can read about Elijah in the Old Testament (1 Kings 17 – 19).

But surely Elijah was a special Holy Joe?

Actually Elijah was flesh and blood just like you and me. But can we really make a difference like Elijah did when we pray? YES, we can, it says so in the Bible, which as we discussed earlier, is God's very own Word. It's as good as if God spoke to you in an audible voice. It is not just an ancient document, it is spiritually alive because God's own Holy Spirit reveals its truth to people – it's God's message to those who seek him.

Even though Jesus is in Heaven now, on his throne sitting at the right-hand side of the Father, receiving all the praise that he is entitled to and more, he is still with us on earth through his representative who Jesus calls the Comforter, who is the Holy Spirit. So when you open up your Bible prepare for a "real" encounter with God. Allow the Holy Spirit to open up your heart and mind to convey your yearnings and thoughts and through the Holy Spirit you will receive answers and guidance from your heavenly Father. As you read God's Word the Trinity is communicating with you! The Father is listening to his Son who is interceding on your behalf as the Holy Spirit is searching your very being and encouraging and helping you to talk to God.

The Holy Spirit is a mystery but no less truthful because of it. Some people get confused at the thought of the third member of the Trinity. The Bible does talk of the Holy Spirit as a person not an impersonal force. It is important to realize this. There is only one God but he is present in three personalities: God the Father, God the Son and God the Holy Spirit. Not a God with three heads like a monster but three distinct personalities. Don't try and work it out; people with bigger brains than you and I have been doing that ever since Jesus ascended to Heaven, 2,000 years ago.

Maybe this analogy will help you. Water can be represented as the flowing transparent stuff that we drink, as steam that tells you that the kettle has boiled, and as ice that complements your Coke on a hot sticky day. But this analogy falls short of describing God, because water would have to be fluid, steam and ice all at the very same time (not in three separate forms) even to touch on how God can be three but exist as one. He is… God!

We have finite minds (limited) while God is infinite (goes on forever). And people say God doesn't exist! How do they know? They only use their little minds. You cannot limit God to time or the dimensions that our world operates in.

We live in a four-dimensional world (the three dimensions of space, plus the dimension of time) but the latest scientific discoveries have established that the equivalent of at least eleven dimensions exist! So just imagine the mind-blowing implications of a personal God who can operate in and beyond such a realm! What cannot be seen or understood from our view would be a simple reality to God! He would certainly have no problem hearing billions of people talking to him at the same time. He would also be able to communicate to all of them individually at the same time!

So, bearing all this heavy stuff in mind, do you really think that God cannot answer all our prayers? So what if those billions of Christians are praying to him all at the same time. He can do what we can't. Don't take Dave Barker's word for it, just listen to what Jesus said about his own Dad, the Creator of everything. "With man this is impossible, but with God all things are possible." Read Matthew 19:16–26 and you will be blessed and blown away when you realize that the Bible is spiritually alive and just how amazing is the God who loves you. Read his Word and pray to him.

Need all this put into modern language so that it is "in ya face"? Okay, here goes: "Word up, stop ya chilling, the Dude of Heaven wants you to switch on your mind's mobile. He's waiting for your call!"

Yeah, I know, I am a middle-aged man trying to be cool. Pray for me! But please get this vital point. When you do, your prayer life will reach higher levels; you'll literally touch Heaven.

▦ You can make a real difference!

Of course, the one thing you do need to be aware of is that prayer really does change you and your circumstances. Just think about Elijah: he was never the same again. When we see God move in response to our prayers, we too can never be the same again. Being a Christian is about being radical. God has to come first. As we decrease he will increase!

GOD MOMENTS

(Listen to what some believers have to say about prayer)

A long-distance call

Jane Holloway, Prayer Co-ordinator for the Evangelical Alliance, is a good friend to *What4* and an authority on the power of prayer. Below, is what she has to say on the subject.

I am so amazed at how God is mobilizing prayer at the moment in the UK. In my role as Prayer Co-ordinator for the Evangelical Alliance, I am in touch with over 360 prayer initiatives all over these islands! I just can't keep up with God in the way he is raising up prayer!

There are young people gathering to pray, church leaders joining and praying together, cities, town, villages and countries; all linked-up with prayer networks. In Wales, they are mobilizing a prayer shield for each of the 1.3 million people who live there. In Scotland, many denominations and churches are involved in an initiative: "Rise up and Pray!" – and they produce a monthly prayer diary for Scotland. Many are continuing to pray and see God answer amid the problems in Northern Ireland.

Sadly, some of the Church is still asleep and hasn't woken up to the vital importance of being in touch with God. This was brought home to me recently.

I was leading a day conference in Felixstowe and teaching on how prayer and evangelism are linked together. I could see that not everyone was with me! Then the church leader came to the front of the church, and she shared how she had just heard the phone ringing and felt prompted to go and answer it, though the office is not normally staffed on Saturday morning.

"Do you pray for people?" was the question at the end of the phone. She replied: "Yes", and then listened to a prayer request for the caller and their family. Thinking this was a local person, she asked the caller from where they were calling? The person replied, "Brighton" and rang off. The whole tone of that conference was changed from that moment on. I imagine that the caller cried out to God, and he knew of our meeting, and he sorted it out for that phone call to get through.

A challenge for all of us – wherever we are – to be ready to listen and to pray as God leads.

Big God – big heart

Sharon Francis is a *What4* team member and has travelled to Uganda to take part in a youth mission. She learned a lot about prayer during this time, and how much God wants us to trust him in all circumstances.

I went on a short-term mission to Uganda with *What4*. While I was there I found that prayer became really important to me. It was essential to spend time with Jesus to get through the day.

I couldn't have managed without God's help. Spending time with God reminded me that I wasn't on my own, but that God was there as well!

Something that God said to me during the prayer times has really stuck with me: "I am a big God with a big heart." This has encouraged me to know that everything is in God's hands.

⠿ How do we pray and what should we pray for?

Quite often we read in the Bible that the disciples asked Jesus: "How do we pray, what should we pray for?" Jesus answers this by teaching them the Lord's Prayer, as we see in Matthew 6. This prayer still applies to Christians today. Read it again and allow God to speak to you because there are so many things that we can pray for, when we realize that God is our Father.

We should pray for everyday things, like our food that we take for granted in the West. Pray for people – including our enemies! A tough one this last one but it is what Jesus asks his disciples to do, even if people have been horrible, mocking and hurtful. It sounds mad, you might think; it goes against natural feelings and the world's way. But remember, we are "born again" when we accept Jesus as our Lord and because the Holy Spirit is dwelling in us, we can call on supernatural strength.

We will not have the cartoon power of Superman, but we will be able to draw on God the Holy Spirit as we make our stands for Jesus. In fact, Jesus says that by turning our other cheek and loving our enemies, we pour live coals on their heads. Imagine that, burning hot stones falling on to your head. This is figurative but it speaks of a spiritual reality: one that will bring shame to the enemies of Jesus. By not reacting in anger and by offering love instead is a real strike at the heart of evil. The shame a person might feel when confronted by a Christian who has been singled out for persecution yet does not react in a hostile way might just bring that persecutor to repentance and conversion.

Praying is practical, even if we are facing hostile or seemingly impossible situations. By these simple acts of obedience and seeking we will please God.

While you are now starting to get excited about the whole reality of prayer, have a look at the amazing fact in capital letters below.

ALL ENERGY COMES FROM GOD

Does it really? God is sovereign. Not like an earthly king or queen. Monarchs do have natural power but God possesses supernatural power. The entire creation came into being because God spoke out his will. There is sin in the world, so does this mean that if God created everything and all energy comes from him he also caused sin? No, God has nothing to do with sin because there is none in him. He did create man though, who sinned at the beginning of his life on earth. Adam and Eve were the sinners, yet if God had not created them they would obviously not have sinned. So it's ultimately God's fault? Of course not! People are to blame for their own sins but God, in his incredible knowledge and power, allows situations and circumstances to run their course, whether the outcome is good or evil. God is always in charge and his plans will never fail.

The world exists because he willed it to. The chemicals and components that make up life are only now in this microscopic age being discovered by brilliant men and women as they seek eternal answers. To many scientists God is a fantasy of primitive man and life is all about luck and survival, but to many other scientists all the advances that are being made in various fields of research and discovery are confirmation of God's wonderful design, his personal signature. Before God spoke creation did not exist, so in this sense all energy comes from him. He deserves all the glory. Read

Genesis 1 and see how many times God spoke the creation into being.

⣿ Up close and personal

God thinks a lot of mankind. In the beginning he made man to rule over his creation (Genesis 1:26), and he also chose to make man in his image (Genesis 1:27). The Old Testament gives accounts of God being in a relationship with specific people as well as the nation of Israel. You only need to look at the Psalms to get an understanding of how close people felt in their relationships with God.

God went further than the Old Testament and saw it was necessary to come to earth himself, to live with us, to walk with us and then to die for us (Romans 5:6–10). Our relationship, our closeness and intimacy with God depends on the Holy Spirit (1 Corinthians 2:10–16).

TO LIVE FULLY WE NEED TO BE IN CONTACT WITH GOD

Diversity in prayer

Tony Campolo (refer to the foreword for more on him) is a friend and a tremendous source of encouragement to *What4*. When it comes to young people the man's heart is BIG. His thoughts on prayer and advice on the different structures we can use when praying makes for interesting reading and will take your pray life up to a higher level. Absorb his words.

It is so easy to make prayer into nothing more than reading off a list of requests! This is not to say that we shouldn't make our requests known to God, but there are several things that I think might be useful to think about:

1. Should we beg the Lord to respond to our prayers? I remember a Catholic nun who was a prayer partner of mine. She would pray for people by pleading with the Lord. Over and over again she would say: "God help that boy. Please, God, help that boy, help that boy." It was very moving to participate in that kind of prayer with her.

2. A second kind of prayer is dead silence. In silence we surrender to God. Prayer is being open to the Holy Spirit. Every morning when I get up, I spend at least ten to fifteen minutes in dead silence. I don't say anything to God. I just make myself open to God and ask that I can hear what God wants to say to me. Allowing God to speak to us through the silence can be another aspect of prayer. When they asked Mother Teresa what she said to God when she prayed, she answered: "I don't say anything, I listen." The next question was: "When you pray what does God say to you?" She answered: "God doesn't say anything. He listens." That's the sort of

praying I'm talking about. This silence is another dimension of prayer.

3. There is a third dimension of prayer that Christians don't often use. We know how to pray for people, but do we know how to pray to people? It's one thing to try to pray for a person by going to God directly, but it's quite another thing when God wants to flow through us to minister to a person. Frank Laubach, in his book on prayer, talks about concentrating on an individual and just allowing the Holy Spirit to be a power flowing through you to that person. It's as though you become a massive lens that focuses the power of God on a particular individual who is in need. A bit like a magnifying glass on a hot sunny day. Some might call this a kind of mental telepathy; I call it prayer telepathy. The God who wants to touch a person moves through us as we focus toward that individual. The person may have a barrier against God, but be open to us, and that's what makes it possible for us to become channels of blessing to others.

Enough already! In the last section we have heard a lot about prayer – let's start being practical and creative about this wonderful tool that God has given us! In the following box we can see that prayer is never boring.

CREATIVE PRAYER

1. Prayer is communication with God. It is our lifeline. (Philippians 4:6, Deuteronomy 4:7)
2. God wants us to corporately and individually lead others in prayer. He desires for us to:

Know his heart for the lost.
Be a house of prayer/temple of the Holy Spirit.
Pray in line with his will.
Use our authority as children of God. (Be brave.)

Your interest in prayer depends on your relationship with God.
Leading others in prayer involves:
Inspiration
Challenge
Passion
Truth

Be Creative
Praying involves using your senses:

Seeing
Reading and praying using Scriptures
Video clips – news/documentaries
Photographs
Banners/murals
Newspapers/Internet/e-mail

Hearing
Music (contemplative or loud)
Listening to other people's experiences
Using the telephone

Doing
Prayer walking
Art and craft
Themed evening events
Fasting and praying
Worshipping
Getting up early to start your day praying to God

Styles of prayer
Declaring God's Word by reading from your Bible
(Ephesians 6:10–20)
One-to-one with God
In pairs
Groups
Praying in different tongues
Praying collectively
Praying silently

Remember these three important points:
1. Don't entertain people! – The purpose of a
prayer evening is to meet and seek God through
prayer.
2. There is a battle being fought, and we can only
enter the war zone with spiritual weapons.
3. Prayer is our God-given mighty weapon! So
let's fight. (2 Corinthians 10:1–4, Ephesians 6:10)

THE PRAYER OF A RIGHTEOUS
PERSON IS POWERFUL!

The life of Jonah (in the Old Testament) is a fine illustration of how prayer changes things. I am sure you know this story well. If you don't, then have a read of the book of Jonah, it's a short account but one that shows us that prayer and trust in God are essential. Not many people find themselves in the belly of a great fish but the Bible says that Jonah experienced this bizarre situation. What about Jonah and his prayer to God? Read about his prayer in Jonah, chapter 2.

Jonah's prayer

I doubt many people would think the stomach of a fish is the ideal place to talk with God. Jonah probably didn't have a whale of a time (forgive the sad sense of humour). But there is so much we can learn from this ancient prophet. Don't forget that the Old Testament is just as powerful and relevant for Christians today.

Jonah's prayer highlights his utter desperation in circumstances that, without God, would have meant dying in the digestive juices of a big fish. As you read of his awful plight in the Bible you can see that he was really thinking about where he had gone wrong. He was truly seeking God, for God was his only hope. Just imagine if God had not given the human race the gift of prayer! Jonah was psychologically and spiritually aware of his sin in disobeying God's command. He would no doubt tell you that being outside of God's will is not a good place to be.

But our God is loving and forgiving, for we then see as we read further on in Jonah that the repentant prophet's prayer turns towards acknowledging God again, and really wanting and desiring to do what God had asked him to do in the first place.

Thank God for his patience!

GOD KNOWS BEST. HE IS ALL-KNOWING, ALL-POWERFUL, ALL-SEEING. YOU CANNOT OUTHINK THE ONE WHO CREATED THOUGHTS!

Prayer is life-changing

"In solemn truth I tell you, anyone believing in me shall do the same miracles I have done, and even greater ones, because I am going to be with the Father. You can ask Him for anything, using my name and I will do it, for this will bring praise to the Father..." (John 14:12–13, Living Bible)

Ask yourself two things:

WHAT DID JESUS DO HERE ON EARTH?

HOW CAN WE DO "GREATER" THINGS?

I have learnt that prayer is life-changing. Prayer can be a positive witness. Applying our beliefs to our actions can affect our prayers. There is diversity in prayer – we can be creative in how we choose to pray! Prayer is paramount to everything we do. Christian charities will tell you that believers' prayers are central to the success of their missions.

Do not be ignorant of this fact: God needs to be the centre of everything that we undertake.

Whatever, wherever and whoever, we must seek God's will first. If we don't, it means we are keeping a little bit of ourselves and not totally surrendering to God. It's not a good idea.

God wants you to receive all he has to offer – that goes for eternity too. You cannot out-receive God, we are finite, and he is infinite. He will always be giving his people more and more. He has planned for eternity – forever! You will not get all that he wants to give you unless you give him all of you. You can start right now. Don't worry if you have been messing up a little bit or a lot, if you are truly sorry and want to start over again, tell God in prayer. And guess what? If you mean it he has already forgiven you. Jesus took that sin on the cross 2,000 years ago. His blood has wiped it away. What a God we know!

Time for a recap

1. Prayer is our mobile communication line to God.

2. Prayer is a powerful and a vital spiritual weapon.

3. Prayer and the Bible are two of the channels that God speaks through.

4. Before we do anything for God we should first always commit it to him through prayer.

5. Without prayer we are useless.

6. We are supposed to be a people of prayer.

🌀 Chapter 2

Give

_____

Q **What For?**

A *So others can receive.*

I'VE GOT NO CASH AND MY HEART'S JUST NOT IN IT.

GIVING IS ABOUT THE ATTITUDE OF THE HEART

How many of us spend time making promises but never actually keep them? Is it because promises mean having to commit yourself to something? It's easy to make a promise but in reality what you have promised can actually mean that you end up doing more than you, well… promised. Jesus said that your yes should be yes and your no should mean no. He told us not to swear by or on things but either to commit to something or not to bother – God wants his disciples to be living radically for him. He does not want a lukewarm people.

"Oh, I'll do that for God but I'll leave the other; at least I'm doing some of what he, um, wants me to do." If you find yourself saying this then you are missing the point of what God wants from you and what God wants to give you. The Christian faith is not something that you can pick and choose from. To be a disciple you have to be prepared to give your all and to receive all that God has for you. Only then can you truly fulfil your part in God's eternal prayer. Don't beat yourself up over your failures but do take them to God in prayer and open your heart to his will.

We are either for him or against him. We either honour him by committing fully, giving him 100 per cent or we give him nothing. Going to church on a Sunday and practising a lovely smile is not enough. Jesus says either be hot (really on fire for him) or cold (stay drowning in the world). See Matthew 5:33–37 and Revelation 3:15. Our God is not a God of compromise. It's all about the attitude of the heart – this in essence is what giving is all about.

God knows that the heart of the problem is the problem of your heart. Sin is the destructive force, which corrupts the heart. Sin is like a sly serpent and once it sinks its poisoned teeth into you, the venom spreads. Your heart then beats to the Devil's tune, leaving you with a wrong attitude, which leads to struggle and strife. This cuts us off from God's will. Only through grace and the Holy Spirit can we overcome.

Throughout the Old Testament, from the time when Moses brought down from the mountain the Ten Commandments that God had given him, God spoke of two commandments that were the root and focus of the whole Law. They were to: "Love the Lord your God with all your heart and with all your soul and with all your strength and with all your mind" and: "Love your neighbour as [you love] yourself." (See Luke 10:27; Leviticus 19:18; and Deuteronomy 6:5.)

When we act on these commandments, our heart learns to reach out and give to others, as God has reached out and given to us. We can only apply love if it is our heart's desire. People can see through false love. Love is pure and transparent, not stained and clothed in darkness. Such love is a gift from God: pray to receive it.

The spirit of giving (Daniel Leakey)

"One of the things that challenged me most was the depth of poverty in Uganda and the people living there. You see the life that people live and it can really pull on the heartstrings. Emotionally it affected me a great deal. But when you look past all that, you really begin to see an amazing attitude of giving and in the love that these people have! Wow, how humbling!"

True giving means our time, talents, possessions and energies. It is more than helping: it is about giving the whole of yourself, not just a part of you; about supporting and loving the person or people whose circumstances have drawn you to them. Do not take being a disciple of Jesus Christ lightly. It is a tremendous privilege to serve the Living God but one day we will all give an account of our lives to Jesus. Praise God that true believers will go to Heaven and share eternity with him, but even so, Christians will be rewarded or not, depending on our stewardship (how we served God on earth). See Matthew 25:14–30. We have an amazing responsibility when we become disciples of Jesus: we are helping him to pave the way for a new Heaven and a new earth, where we will reign with him.

If it sounds all too good to believe, then get

into your Bible: read through Isaiah 64 of the Old Testament; Mark 13 and Matthew 24; the letters of Paul, 1 Thessalonians 4:13–18 and chapter 5, also 2 Thessalonians 1 and 2; see Revelation 21 and 22 and the descriptions of what it will be like in eternity; go and buy books written about the different books of the Bible that will help you explain them better; get a Bible commentary. Remember, in order to start giving your all to God and the coming kingdom, you have to be in constant prayer and always reading his Word; because once you know his will it transforms your desire and you will not be able to stop yourself from giving the whole of yourself for the glory of God.

The Bible truly is our sword and shield (Hebrews 4:12). Many followers of Jesus Christ know all about giving their all – being a Christian for many people in the past and today means paying the ultimate cost: giving their lives in order for others to be saved and rescued from Hell (a place without God).

As you read in the previous chapter, God doesn't ask of us anything he hasn't already done. He proved it when his Son died for the sins of the world. John 3:16 tells us of the magnitude of love that God has for the people of the world and the planet that he created, when he gave his only Son, Jesus, so that we could be saved from Hell: an eternity without him where only torment awaits for ever. "For God so loved the world that he gave his one and only Son, that whoever believes in him shall not perish but have eternal life."

This one verse has often been referred to as "the Gospel in a nutshell", because it sums up the very heart of the message that tells of God's incredible plan for the people that love him. In giving the world the Lord Jesus, God's very heart is revealed. And it shows that God's heart of love for mankind was a driving force in the sacrificing of Jesus. Just take some time to close your eyes, bow your head and meditate on God's love. When you find yourself saying, wow: what love! you will start to love others, as you love yourself.

It is all down to the attitude of our heart when it comes to giving: whether to others or to God.

Giving time to God

It's always good to hear personal testimonies and thoughts on subjects pertaining to God; because it encourages us and sheds light on sometimes difficult concepts. Emma Ridgewell was on *What4*'s Motiv8 (a year-out scheme) and here are her thoughts about the subject of giving.

I wonder what you are thinking after reading the heading above?
Maybe you're expecting a lecture on how Christians should wake up every day at 4.30am to spend at least three solid hours in prayer. Cut out all TV, spend less time with friends and generally

master the art of developing extremely pale skin due to the amount of time spent in your room waiting for God to speak to you! That might work for some people – please tell me who?

Giving time to God could be, on the other hand, a bit like being married. Hopefully you would not spend just three hours talking to your husband or wife every day (which would soon decrease to about two minutes, by the way) and then forget that you're even married to them for the rest of the time. A good marriage involves a couple consistently giving time to each other, even if they are not in the same room. A couple may be apart due to work or an activity that only one is involved in but it still shouldn't stop the husband and wife thinking of each other.

Giving time to God should be something we enjoy, that comes naturally to us within everyday life. After all, it is the way God wants it to be.

Sometimes it's good to set aside a specific time to be spent with God, but if we become too ritualistic about having to keep to set deadlines, this usually ends up in us feeling guilty when we can't stick to our plans. Eventually this can result in us becoming angry towards God and developing a false impression of who he is. God wants us to enjoy being loved by him, to smile when he speaks to us, to be able to feel ecstatic joy in His presence when everything around us in the world is in chaos and misery.

When we reach this stage, time becomes no object and we can't get enough of being with God because we are falling more and more in love with him. If there is just one thing worth investing the majority of your time in – that has to be time for God. For *"His divine power has given us everything we need for life and godliness through our knowledge of him who called us by his own glory and goodness"* (2 Peter 1:3).

Whatever your position in life, if Jesus is the centre, all your time will be given to him without your even realizing it.

Emma sums up well the fact that if we are giving our "all" to God and he is the centre of our lives, then finding time to be with God will become not a discipline but a pleasure. We will not realize because every aspect of our lives will be devoted to him – whatever we are doing.

When giving is mentioned, cash immediately springs to mind, but though the submitting of our finances to God's purpose is important, the concept of giving involves so much more.

Can you imagine how big a difference we can all make if our different abilities, talents and skills are combined in order to give to God? Remember he wants all of us. After all God is the one who gave us our various accomplishments in the first place. He is not a killjoy, in fact the opposite. He wants us to enjoy and use them for his glory.

God is not on an ego trip, whatever scoffers say. He is the Creator and simply knows best. And the beautiful thing about aligning our thoughts and desires with his is that our lives will be enhanced because we will be utilizing our gifts in the way they were designed to be used and the purpose for which they were made – to worship God.

This way we will actually be living life to the full and as believers we get to do that forever! It is ironic to think that by surrendering to God we are truly set free. To the world this is a contradiction, but to a people who have had their spiritual eyes opened it is a brilliant truth. And that is what God does – he opens our closed eyes to spiritual truths and then helps us to keep them from shutting again.

Take to heart this wonderful fact: for true disciples of Jesus Christ there are no such words as losers or second-raters. God's Kingdom is for winners. If you surrender all areas of your life to him you can claim the eternal victory that Jesus has already won for his people on the cross 2,000 years ago. If we fall in with God's desire and do what he asks, we simply cannot lose – he assures our victory. Be aware: he gives us the choice to receive his victory not. Ask yourself: do you truly want to claim Jesus' spoils of war? If you do then the most amazing life awaits you now and in the age to come. If you choose to be apathetic to the one who took the nails and had a spear thrust into his side for his people; the one that gave up his rightful place in paradise in order to know what it is like to be flesh and bone and ultimately to save all those that will come to him, and recognize him as God in a human body, then the choice is yours. Whatever your decision there is a price to pay.

1. To follow him is not easy, there is and will be times of hardships, even death.
2. There will be great reward on earth and in Heaven for his people, the true disciples.
3. To walk away and reject him means there will be no prizes and one day, the Bible says, those people's teeth will grind together and their cries will be heard for all eternity (Matthew 13:41–43) as they realize whom they rejected when they had their time on earth.

Take some time out to bow your head and reflect on God's holiness. It will be sobering and humbling, even scary. After a while look up with expectant and hungry eyes to the treasures and wonders that God has in store for you. And as you praise him tell him how much you love him, because his love for you is immeasurable.

Kenya drought

We hear many stories from charities working abroad in continents like Asia and Africa. These accounts illustrate how important the gift of giving really can be. In a moment you will read a wonderful story from Kenya, about the struggle of one particular local group that became news to the rest of the people in that country.

The Turkana people in northern Kenya have been struggling to survive a severe drought, which has led to terrible hardship for years on end. Sadly, many news reporters can become hardened to suffering. But when a Christian charity flew some of Kenya's national press to see the effect of the drought for themselves, they were staggered and were determined to do something about it. So they used their journalistic talents to publicize the terrible situation and appealed for help.

Wilfred Kiboro of The National Media Group reported:

What we found shocked us. We wanted to establish the facts for ourselves. We found that some had died and many were at risk of starvation. That's why we decided to highlight the plight of the Turkana people.

Readers were deeply moved by the scale of this human disaster. Many of the Turkana livestock had been destroyed by famine. The people had walked for hours to reach a clinic and to seek out food; their frail bodies were dressed in shabby, torn clothes – they had nothing.

We wanted our readers to see their responsibility for helping their own people and so we appealed for funds. We were surprised to see offers of help pouring in. However, the appeal raised not only money but also practical help such as clothes and medicines.

But this still left one problem – how to get the aid to those in need. To travel the 500 miles by road from Nairobi to Lodwar would take two days and would mean going through bandit country. Thanks to a UK charity we were able to provide flights to deliver these vital emergency supplies and medicines.

So many people gave in different ways. The journalists gave their skills; their readers gave food, clothes and medicines. Pilots gave their time and the giving of Christians in the UK enabled the flights to happen. The terrible situation of the Turkana was far too big for one person to solve, but with many people giving what they could, help and relief became possible.

What Wilfred says is so true. We do not all possess the same gifts, but we do all have certain gifts, and when we join them all together we become a powerful body. This is what Paul means when we read in 1 Corinthians 12 about the Body of Christ (the Church).

We all have a role in the building of God's kingdom. We have no excuses, because God has equipped us all with the tools for the job. The account that Wilfred relayed proves that. Wilfred's gift was journalism and he chose to use his specialist field to highlight a worthy cause. Wilfred had a giving heart. By lending his natural skills he gave the opportunity for his readers to give financially and in other ways to the plight of suffering people. When Christians join together to show the world the Truth via word and practical application, great things are achieved. God has given to us so that we can give to others. Being an exclusive people is not what Jesus wants us to be: Christ's disciples are supposed to care, share and dare.

Ultimate giving

Sometimes giving is easy, but when the circumstances are hazardous God may be asking us for more than our money and skills!

The SAS (Special Air Service) embraces the motto "Who Dares Wins". Okay, so does Derek Trotter from the TV comedy *Only Fools and Horses*, but seriously, as disciples of Jesus Christ in this new 21st century we are going to have to be brave when we make our stands.

There will be times when friends will not want to know you because you are acting weird and freaky. But Jesus wants you to give your all to his cause. Perhaps a Christian's motto should be "Who Has Faith Has Won", because it is imperative that we should never forget: Jesus has already won the war – he asks us just to trust in him. There are many battles still left to fight. Some are extremely dangerous, and we will be outnumbered at times, but we have an invincible arsenal of weapons: prayer, the Word and our gifts. And just think, we have the three greatest Field Marshals (the highest military rank you can achieve) planning our strategies: God the Father, God the Son and God the Holy Spirit. The final victory is assured – Jesus fought and won it 2,000 years ago. The enemy is defeated and on the retreat.

When I write of war, battles and victory I am not focusing on spiritual warfare. Of course this is a reality and a vital part of what being a Christian is all about. In this instance though, I am drawing a parallel with the horrific though natural conflict of the Second World War and our standing as disciples in this new millennium. As we read earlier, giving is about more than the releasing of our finances – it is about giving everything for God: our very bodies, hearts, souls and sometimes lives. War is a terrible time, but it is during such circumstances, amongst the terror, dirt and bullets, that there is incredible bravery, sacrifice and giving of the ultimate kind.

During the Second World War, in June 1944, the Allies (the countries of the world which united to defeat Hitler's army and to fight the Japanese in South East Asia) stormed the beaches of northern France. It was the beginning of the end for Hitler's evil dream of world domination. From that moment on he had lost the war.

The Allies had great leaders in Winston

Churchill, Montgomery and Eisenhower who inspired morale and the hope that in the end victory would be assured. Sadly, more people in London lost their lives in the last months of the war in Europe than during the Blitz at the beginning, because of Hitler's last-ditch attempt in ordering his army to send over a lethal pilotless flying bomb called the V1 rocket, more commonly known as the "doodlebug". Who would have thought, after all the years of fighting and the bombing of London at the start of the war, that the number of civilian deaths would be greater at the end? And the actual war did not cease until the Japanese surrendered in 1945.

You see, even though victory is ultimately ours, we have to go on fighting to the end of our lives. It's like reading a book – you know the last page has been written, but to understand the ending you have to read the rest of the book first.

We can draw parallels with the Second World War when we consider the whole subject of giving beyond money. Firstly, for believers in Christ the war has been won but there are many battles left to win in Christ's name – sometimes it will mean the loss of lives (just think of the persecuted Church) and certainly there will be suffering. History has proved that followers of Christ will not have an easy life. The Christian walk is demanding.

Many men, women and children gave their lives during the Second World War. In fact, without their sacrifices we would not be living in the free society of today that we have enjoyed for the last 60 years. Today many of our brothers and sisters are dying for Christ's Kingdom. These believers live in countries where Christianity is thought to be an abomination. Just like in the last world war where people died for the hope of future peace for others, so some disciples of Christ will have to pay the ultimate price for the kingdom coming.

There will be battles where the enemy will simply roll over and surrender, but there will also be long drawn-out fights with heavy losses! Again we are not discussing spiritual warfare as such but everyday circumstances. A battle could be standing up for Jesus in the classroom when everyone else is laughing, or maybe your parents or brothers and sisters are giving you a hard time, or the fact that some of your friends don't want to know you unless you drop the "Jesus talk". These are very real earthly battles for young Christians. Do not take them lightly – God doesn't, he knows the ones who are for him. The good news is we have an awesome trio of "Holy" field marshals behind us. With respect to those great men of the Second World War, our leaders put them in the shade. After all, God knew the leaders of the Allies of the Second World War before they were born!

We have the Father whose will is our victory; the Son who led by example by sacrificing all he had to storm the enemies' strongholds and defeat Satan; the Holy Spirit who represents the Son on earth and applies the power of God to the soldiers of Christ – we cannot lose, as long as we realize a good soldier obeys his commanders!

What a fantastic difference we can make when we give. But I wonder what would happen if we chose not to give? We can see when we look at the world that it has suffered the effects of not giving enough. We are constantly reminded that one third of its population lives in great prosperity, as compared to two thirds that live in desperate poverty!

There is a well-known saying that sums up the underlying cause for the great difference between those that have and those that have not. It runs: "There is enough in the world for everyone's need, but not enough for everyone's greed!"

God has made enough provision for all of his creation, but it is our sin and greed that leaves two thirds of the world in poverty. A sad example of this was the government of Ethiopia in the 1980s. After charity events like Live Aid where the rock and pop stars of that time joined together for two unprecedented concerts played in the UK and the

USA to raise money for the victims of Ethiopia, it was reported later that a lot of the money/aid raised was hijacked by government soldiers and instead of helping the dying it lined the pockets and stomachs of the wealthy. Greed is a terrible thing. But the wonderful news is that by giving, we protect our hearts from greed, and in our own small way, we can help to bridge the poverty gap.

When you read this next illustration about giving, you will be overwhelmed by the whole concept of giving to others: you will see the difference it makes.

I met a young man (I'll call him Tough Guy) who was one of these real hard lads. At fifteen he had a terrible reputation. I had the privilege of going into his school and taking an assembly. The subject I chose was "the needs of other countries". I did not speak to Tough Guy personally but he was moved by something that I spoke about to his fellow pupils.

Two weeks later I returned to the school to teach a RE lesson. Tough Guy approached me. He still had that laddish swagger – you know the type – but he was clutching an envelope. Inside of it was £22: a donation to help the people that I had spoken about. He raised the money by baking cakes! Who said image was everything? No one was more surprised than his mum – she was stunned. He was giving his time, skill (well, have you tried baking a cake?) and energy to helping others less fortunate than himself. Tough Guy had become Nice Guy; he was exemplifying what giving is all about.

In James chapter 1, we see that God gives generously and graciously to us all. Hey, just take a look at the countryside to see the natural wonders he has made, and that is just for starters...

Time please!

Daniel Leakey shares his thoughts on giving our time to God, and how God can use this beyond what we can expect.

Am I giving or am I forgetting? Do other people really need me to tell them about Jesus? Surely I don't need to give up the little spare time I have? After all, there are plenty of outreach teams all geared up for that sort of thing.

Have you ever thought any of those things? I know I have. Then God reminded me of Jonah. Okay, so maybe God won't have me swallowed by a great fish. (Then again, maybe he will!) But God told Jonah to give up his time to go to Nineveh and spread the word because the people really needed to hear it. I decided that if

God wanted me somewhere then he definitely had a good reason for it.

Giving up even a little time for Jesus can go a long way. God knows what will happen to people's lives when you give your time to speak to the young people in the youth group, or the homeless man in town. He knows what will happen when you give your time and help to build a church in the middle of a jungle somewhere. You might never know what your prayers, money or talking about a project has achieved but somewhere you have touched someone's life and changed it for the better.

Don't forget the people who need to hear. Give a little time, because one day it will run out!

"I'm setting you up as a light for the nations, so that my salvation becomes global!" (Isaiah 49:6, *The Message*).

Chain reaction

Here is another uplifting example of giving. It comes from a charity that carries out the Lord's work in Tanzania. It shows how important the supporter's role is. This particular charity provided a much-needed aeroplane to reach remote parts of that country. Again we see how the Body of Christ has different functions. After all without supporters the charities will not exist and without the charities, help will not be available. A chain of people will lead to a chain of events and when God is in control, exciting times are ahead.

Each month a Cessna 206 forms one link in the chain of another partnership that makes a big difference.

The aircraft dedicates three days to "safari flying", taking five nurses and their equipment to run clinics in isolated places. The nurses are essential in villages where diseases that are easily treatable in the West can spread and become life threatening.

But when we talk of clinics, please dispel any notions of white buildings with modern facilities and comfortable waiting rooms. In the village of Yaida Chini, its clinic is held under a tree – because the branches provide relief from the heat. There used to be a basic building, but an earthquake destroyed it. Thank God that we live in a country that only sees major natural disasters via the TV screen. Sadly, Africa suffers continually.

Needy locals walk for miles through the bush to reach their only source of medical help. Again we experience the working of God's chain. The charity reports the situation; the supporters learn about it and contribute the desperately needed finance; the charity then can purchase a plane; the nurses can then be flown into the hot spot and the villagers then receive healing because God's people are distributing their gifts and seeking God's guidance. Every link is paramount to the operation's success.

You may not find yourself in such a dramatic situation but just by telling your neighbour, or the person sitting next to you at school or on the bus, about Jesus can be the beginning of another one of God's thousands of chains. You are an important part of God's plan and coming kingdom.

Giving has a positive impact on other people, as we join together for a common cause the impact grows and touches many more people; and with God at the helm, our giving multiplies. This is because God will use whatever we give for his eternal plan and purpose, but we'll have to wait until we reach Heaven to see just how much difference our giving has really made.

YOU'VE GOT TIME TO GIVE SOME TIME TO OTHERS.

Be stretched in giving

Ruth Box shares her views on what it means to give to God.

(Beware, you'll have to have a brain the size of a planet to work the heading out!) So you reckon that you should "give". It sounds quite holy – can't you just hear yourself saying, "Oh yes, I give to God regularly." But what does that actually mean? Is it something to do with the collection plate at church on a Sunday? And why should you "give", whatever give means?

Let's have a look at a bit of the New Testament. Find 2 Corinthians 8:1–15. This passage is part of a letter that one of Jesus' top guys, Paul, wrote to a church in a place called Corinth, in Greece. Paul is holding up a group of people from Macedonia as an example to the Church in Corinth, because they were really good at giving. You'll notice from the letter that these guys were not rich – they were just giving. So let's dig a bit into this subject and try and answer some questions.

What does it mean to give?

To give means that you're passing something on without expecting to gain anything from the gift – you're making a present of whatever it is you're giving.

Also, yielding is quite a good image to have in your mind when you think about giving something to God. If you yield something you give it up completely: no conditions, no strings, no defences – you become completely vulnerable if you yield to someone or something.

It's pretty obvious from what we have just read that the person you give to is God, usually through what you give to other people, but the ultimate direction and recipient of your gift is God. That makes the idea of giving an awful lot easier. It's easy to give something to someone you love: but God should be your first love. Just think what he has given you. If you need a reminder take a quick look at verse 9, "For you know the grace of our Lord Jesus Christ, that though he was rich, yet for your sakes he became poor, so that you through his poverty might become rich."

But how do you give to God?

Well, you can't package up a few five-pound notes or dollar bills and stick them in the first-class post to Heaven; I'm pretty sure of this. But you can give or share what you have with other people: this is how God asks us to give to him. Check out verse 5 and you'll notice that the Macedonian guys yielded their lives to God, and then out of that decided to give money to Paul and his team to help them. Obviously God had prompted them through the Holy Spirit to do this by putting the idea in their minds. The other thing that's really important about how you give is the way you feel about it. You need to give willingly and, the Bible says, cheerfully! Look at verses 3 and 12. You can see that it was people's willingness to give that was important, rather than how much they gave.

So you've decided to give to God. What can you give?

Basically, God wants us to give him whatever we have: money, time, talents, possessions, love, practical help – the list goes on and is repeated elsewhere in this book. But if we, the 21st-century disciples of Jesus Christ, committed these principles to our Christian walk we would see God move in mightier ways. The first rule of thumb is to be willing to share whatever you have with others. Don't get stressed into trying to give what you don't have – e.g. if you can't sing for toffee, don't offer to entertain the residents of your local old folks' home with your rendition of Robbie's greatest hits! Look at verses 2 Corinthians 8:13–15 and you'll get the idea. You might also notice that it works both ways. When you're prepared to give what you have when you have it, you'll find that others will be prompted to give to you when you're in need. God's good that way!

When should you give?

The most important answer to the above question is whenever God tells you to. Listen to what he is saying to you – you will know because certain thoughts won't go away. Hear him as you read your Bible; even simply through noticing that someone needs something that you can help them with. But giving is not restricted to putting your small change in the collection plate on a Sunday morning – you can even give by letting one of your friends have first go on your PlayStation; or by not giving your teacher such a hard time in class! (Radical stuff, eh.)

So there you go – a few ideas to get you started on the route to giving. There are lots more examples in the Bible of people giving to God. Why not get hold of a concordance (a big book listing all the subjects in the Bible), look up "giving" and follow the references to find some of the stories?

Here's a starter story for you in Mark 6:30–44. Ask yourself: Who did the giving? What did he give? What did Jesus do with his gift? What was the result? How would you have felt if it had been you that had done the giving? You can experience those exact same feelings if you're willing to give what you have to God – so what are you waiting for? Get out there and. GIVE.

Giving is all about our attitude. But if someone were to ask you, what is the greatest gift you can give to someone, the answer would have to be – Jesus! God the Father gave the world his only Son; Jesus sacrificed his life for all those who would come to him. He gave us every part of him, he poured out his blood so that we can now approach the throne of God boldly and receive his forgiveness and gift of eternal life. Because of the Lord's death and resurrection and his sending of the Holy Spirit, we can now give the gift of Jesus and his saving love to others – the lost who don't know him… yet!

One of the greatest outreach projects ever has been a movie – the Jesus Film, which is a straightforward, well-acted portrayal of Luke's Gospel. It has been translated into many languages (in Uganda alone there are more than 40 languages!) and has been shown in hundreds of villages throughout Africa. This film has become a powerful tool for preaching God's Word. Remote communities have the opportunity to see the Bible come to life. Forget multiplex cinemas! Sometimes the film is shown in community halls, but more often than not it is likely to be played via a powered diesel generator projecting on to a sheet that is fastened between two trees. It is one form of evangelism that has had a life-changing effect on thousands of people.

Sam Tsapwe, a charity worker and IT assistant in Uganda, closes down his computer on Friday evenings and begins thinking how he can share Jesus that night with others.

Sam's commitment to showing the *Jesus Film* has resulted in many great things happening. Since a recent visit by Sam to a village called Mbale, local pastors have set up a group of evangelists who have been visiting other villages and towns and God has really honoured their hunger for his Son. Two new churches have been established and many villagers have become Christians. Sam is thrilled with the response:

"We praise God for open doors in this area and for the workers willing to go out in His name!"

Sam is just one of thousands of Christians around the world doing his bit for God's Kingdom. Many witness in countries where Christianity is barely tolerated and when it is there are restrictions like: "do not try and convert others, keep it behind closed doors… "

In other countries our brothers and sisters in Christ are mocked, despised and even killed. What started with the murder of Jesus two millennia ago continues today with his 21st-century followers. We are so blessed to be living in the West where all we face is derision at worst. Let this fact motivate us: our brothers and sisters around the world are facing hostility, pain and abuse everyday because they choose to follow the King of kings, let us not have any shame when we are confronted with opposition to the hope that we have. Read Hebrews 13:3 because there are Christians in peril at this very moment! "Remember those in prison as if you were their fellow-prisoners, and those who are ill-treated as if you yourselves were suffering."

We should praise God that he has placed us where we are. In the UK and other affluent countries we have an abundant choice of Bible translations; a competitive Christian music industry; books that aid us in understanding God's Word; and modern church buildings. Most of us have a nice home and a job; we even get to take holidays. Now all this in itself is a good thing – people have fought wars and made sacrifices so that we can enjoy the quality of life that we experience, but let's not forget the parts of the "Body" that are living in terrible situations.

Don't beat yourselves up over your

comparative luxury, God has a plan for you right where you are – and it is an important and crucial one: the lost live in the West too!

But how can we give to our brothers and sisters outside our safety circles? Firstly we must pray for them – always! We can support charities like Open Doors who take Bible materials into "dangerous anti-Christian countries" (perhaps God is calling you to join an Open Doors team or a similar organization?). We can give people information about the suffering Church, statistics and facts that the Western media do not bother to report on.

In 1999, 164,000 Christians died as martyrs for Jesus, and the number are increasing! (See the two boxes below.) Their crime: they showed the Creator's love to the world but the created returned hate, culminating in murder. This stark reality should make us seek to honour God more: continually to be in his Word and in prayer – and to give our all in every situation for his glory. Never be ashamed of the Gospel: God gave it to us through the death of his Son, so that we could be set free forever. One day we will reign in Heaven with him, but until then let's give all that we have to the pursuit of saving the lost through the love we have been given. We are not alone: we have the Father and Son in Heaven and the Holy Spirit dwelling in us. And of course, fellow Christians are also fighting this spiritual war; so come on, let's give the world what we ourselves have been given!

See the box below to see what is meant by the ultimate sacrifice. Though we cannot know for sure how the apostles died, owing to a lack of historical documentation, we do know that many of the early Christians were persecuted, tortured and murdered.

According to tradition the apostles are thought to have died for the Faith in the following way:

Philip: Death by stoning, AD 54

Barnabas: Death by burning, AD 64

Peter: Crucified, Rome, AD 69

Paul: Beheaded, Rome, AD 69

Andrew: Crucified, Achaia, AD 70

Matthew: Beheaded, Ethiopia, AD 70

Luke: Hanged, Greece, AD 93

Thomas: Speared to death, Calamino, AD 70

Mark: Dragged to death, Alexandria, AD 64

James (The Less): Clubbed to death, Jerusalem, AD 63

John: Abandoned, Isle of Patmos, AD 63

(Extract from the Evidence Bible, Bridge Logos: Ray Comfort)

Faith unto death

"I have no personal friends at school. But you know what? I am not going to apologize for speaking the name of Jesus. I am not going to justify my faith to them, and I am not going to hide the light that God has put into me. If I have to sacrifice everything, I will take it. If my friends have to become my enemies for me to be with my best friend, Jesus, then that's fine with me."

Rachel Scott, Columbine martyr

"Now I have given up on everything else. I have found it to be the only way to really know Christ and to experience the mighty power that brought Him back to life again, and to find out what it means to suffer and die with Him. So, whatever it takes I will be one who lives in the fresh newness of life of those who are alive from the dead."

Cassie Bernall, 17, Columbine martyr

(Extract from the Evidence Bible, Bridge Logos: Ray Comfort)

When we reflect on the reality of suffering for Christ, and the brothers and sisters who have died rather than deny him, it should challenge us. Praise God that we live in such blessed times where we are not looking over our shoulders for enemies of Jesus as we gather together for worship and

Bible study. But it does not mean that we just sit back like the world and enjoy the comforts of freedom of religion and forget that God has a kingdom to build. We should realize this fact every day and dedicate ourselves to whatever God has planned for us as individuals. We should continually praise our heavenly Father for the time he has chosen for us to walk his earth. Let's make the use of these precious days and the climate of freedom that we enjoy to further Christ's cause.

When a disciple faces death it really is that Christian's faith on the line, at that moment he or she is a breath away from eternity. Stories of martyrs humble and stir us with a passion to go for it for our Lord and Saviour. Deaths of fellow Christians who have chosen to stand for Christ right up until the end bring home what being a true believer is all about. It is like having a cold shower in the middle of an amazing, pulsating worship concert. Imagine, there you are in a packed stadium singing and swaying to the sound of the band, making bold declarations of your never-ending faith, and that you will always stand, no matter what. Then all of a sudden the sky sends down freezing cold water onto the crowd, and a booming voice shouts from Heaven a list of names. They are the thousands of disciples who gave their lives for Christ. Then the voice tells us of all the people who right now are suffering because of their love for God. Would you still sway with your hands in the air and make such bold declarations like you did before the cold shower? Or would the band stop playing and lead you and the rest of the crowd out of the stadium and into the dark areas of the world where Christ's light only flickers?

There is so much more to being a Christian than living an endless guilt trip, but it is good for the soul to reflect on the fact that Christ wants us to be prepared to give him everything. The calling may be dramatic or pragmatic, the one thing it won't be is for anyone to be static. So if you think you have had your head in the clouds, just gone along with the flow; you've read and sung about what you are supposed to be doing, even passionately telling others what they should be doing, but you know that you have not been giving your all, then come back down to earth because you are needed – God's army can't operate to its full capacity if a soldier has gone AWOL.

Giving is practical

We have learned that giving is rewarding and makes a major difference: both to the giver and to the receiver. But now we need to be practical. Yes, this world's system runs on that word "money". Yes, true Christian giving means the attitude of your heart but it also requires parting with your cash and for some people it will mean tightening the purse strings and changing the way you live.

This world is choking because we are driven by consumerism and obsessed with material quantity. "It's new therefore I want it!" You may not actually use it but at least you will be up there with the neighbours and your friends. Well, I have news for you: going with the crowd is not what being a disciple of Jesus is all about. He calls for a radical people who are to be salt and light to the world (Matthew 5:13–16). Salt is for flavouring: we should taste different to non-believers.

Yes, they might want to spit you out but that's not the point – Jesus never promised that everyone would like you. After all, the Bible says the people of the world are walking around in spiritual darkness: we should light up their path when we come in contact with them. Again they might not like to see our shine because it exposes the true them, but Jesus told us not to hide the light he has given us – so get mixing with the lost: give them the flavour of the Saviour and turn their night into light.

The message of our faith is not popular to the world. In all we do we must be humble and show genuine love to everyone we know and meet. We are called to be different, and even though as Christians we are adopted by God and know that we have the meaning to life, we still need to remember we do not deserve our inheritance, we can never earn it. It is vital to keep this at the front of our minds and apply it to all that we do, because then we will resist being arrogant. All that we possess in Christ is because of God's amazing grace! See Ephesians 2:8–9.

Giving money to God

Why should we have to part with our hard-earned money and give it to God? This might be a difficult concept to grasp for those of us living in the abundant West. If God is the Creator of the universe and he owns everything – including us – then does he really need our money?

This is a fair question. But we have to go beyond the flesh – much further than our grey brain cells. We have to start seeing through spiritually opened eyes – the way that God sees it.

In previous chapters we have learnt that God talks to us through his Word and prayer, so you might find yourself seeking him through these two channels in order to understand why we should give our money to him. By the way he is not asking for all of it, but he does desire his people to be cheerful givers. The Jews of the Old Testament would give God the first fruits of their harvests – ten per cent of their produce. Many Christians use this as rule of measure today. God does want us to be cheerful givers, not due to compulsion but because we truly want to (2 Corinthians 9:7). Some may think that God is a bit greedy. Yet, this unfair description of him doesn't resonate with other parts of his character.

So let us look at it another way – the command to give this amount was not for God's benefit but for ours. So, if this is true how do we give him our money? You will not be surprised by now to know the answer is in his Word. In Deuteronomy 26 it says that we should give our offering to the Levites, the stranger, the fatherless and the widow (Levites were the chosen group of people in Israel who worked in the temple – the equivalent of modern day pastors, ministers and church workers).

Just to prove that God is not greedy for money he doesn't expect us to go to the bank, withdraw a certain amount, pile it on the floor and watch it miraculously disappear as the hand of God invisibly snatches it way. Our God may well move supernaturally but a lot of the times he likes to keep it practical and "normal". Okay, so how can we do that?

Today we can give to God via our church – just look at your church as an established mission station – and to various charities who exist to help and support the less privileged. Many people give through the channels such as Gift Aid or covenants, where the tax can be recovered. This helps people give certain amounts where tax is not paid.

The command to give is no modern-day idea. God issued it over 3,000 years ago before there was a social security service run by the government. So can we argue that we no longer need to give in the same way because we now have a welfare system that helps the unemployed and the poor, but back then, in biblical days, they did not have such an agency? A moment's thought will tell you this is nonsense. Just take a look at how many charities exist to carry out their vital work because people contribute to their cause. Of course we have to give today. There are plenty, millions of people both at home and overseas that need help.

Jesus said: "The poor you will always have with you…" (Matthew 26:11). And true to his word he was right – we do.

There is so much more to giving than just helping others, essential and important as this is. The Bible talks about giving as being part of our thankfulness and worship to God, and stresses that the attitude in which we give is more important than what we give. (This should sound familiar, check out the story about the widow's offering, Luke 21:1–4). To paraphrase 1 Corinthians 13 it says: "If I give everything I own to the poor and even go to the stake to be burned as a martyr, but I don't love, then I have got nowhere."

If we love God then we will want to please him. And God loves it when we help others. When you think that God has given us everything that we possess, then the idea of sharing a portion of it is not so strange. Think of the Christian charities, organizations, churches and suffering people who will benefit from it. God is so fair. In financial terms he only wants ten per cent. You will truly find that the old saying: "it is more blessed to give than to receive" rings true.

So even in parting with some of our money we gain! What other form of spending brings such a "spiritual dividend"? Sure, buying those clothes you so wanted brings you a kind of superficial happiness, but clothes or whatever cannot last forever. However, God rewards for eternity for the things we do in "real" love on earth. You cannot fool God with false offerings, and you cannot outgive him, but you can participate in the building of his kingdom and giving is one of the ways that his amazing plan will be fulfilled.

Time for a recap

1. God has chosen Christians to give to his cause.
2. God's Kingdom will not be built unless we give.
3. Giving means being prepared to give our all.
4. What we give is what was given to us by God.
5. God doesn't want all our money. He just wants us to give some of it.
6. When you give yourself to God with a loving heart you will be eternally rewarded.

⟲ Chapter 3

Go

Q What For?

A *Because the lost need to be found.*

Big world – big God

Michelle Sainsbury is a youth leader. She reflects on the wonder of our God.

I was sitting in the middle of a village on the steps of a house looking over some mountains and I thought to myself: What a big world it is and what a huge God we have, who has created such a place! At this point, I felt two completely different feelings: initially I felt negative; I thought I was too insignificant to do anything and that I had no part to play in God's plan; but then I came to realize that I had God with me and with him I could do great and wonderful things for him!

I agree with Michelle, it is a big world and God wants us to catch a fresh glimpse of his reality – to see just how big this world really is, but even more – to see and comprehend that God is so much bigger! When our vision of God grows, so too will our vision for the world and the part he wants us all to play.

When Michelle Sainsbury travelled to Ethiopia with *What4*'s first mission team in 1994, little did she realize how much this experience would change her outlook on life and her view of God. Read again Michelle's words in the box above: you can never be insignificant when you become a disciple of Jesus – you have a major part to play. Believe it! God does not lie. Out there is a big world with great needs, but with God we can make a big difference.

✳ The starfish story

One day, while a man was out walking on a beach just after a storm, he saw a young boy picking up starfish from the beach and throwing them back into the sea.

The man asked the boy why he was doing this? There was no way he could possibly save all the thousands of starfish that had been washed up because of the storm. The young boy picked up a starfish, turned to the man and said: "Because it makes a difference to this one!" And with that he turned and tossed the starfish back into the ocean.

God is a God of the "individual" as well as the "thousands".

Check out Luke 15:7 "I tell you that in the same way there will be more rejoicing in Heaven over one sinner who repents than over ninety-nine righteous persons who do not need to repent." That one person who is saved is so important to God that there is a celebration in Heaven!

If you think that being a Christian and following Jesus is predictable and boring, then you are probably going after the wrong Jesus! The radical life of Christ on earth demonstrated a lifestyle that was unpredictable; so much so that Jesus took the enemy by storm. The Devil could not defeat Jesus in the desert wilderness and the religious leaders could not silence the truth he spoke – he was a brilliant philosopher and theologian, and the grave of death could not hold him!

It is in God's power that we go out into the world. The very same power that won the victory at Calvary – Christ is with us; every footstep, every prayer; through all life can throw at us, Jesus is standing there with us.

God calls us to be missionaries from day one of our salvation. The word mission means to carry out a specific duty. A Christian missionary's duty is to go into the world with the message of the Gospel, and to lead people to Christ. The thought of a person going to some faraway land with a Bible in their hand, and dressed in Victorian clothes is a non-churched view. Thousands of Christians are still called to take the Gospel overseas, where they will find hostility towards Jesus' message from the locals. But being a missionary is what all believers in Christ are, whether in their own town, village or city, school, workplace or home. Being a missionary is simply being a Christian – you don't need to travel to acquire the title. You are a missionary wherever God has placed you on the earth and whatever business, occupation or situation you find yourself in – our mission is to be a witness to the claims of Jesus Christ.

Look how God speaks to Isaiah: "Whom shall I send? And who will go for us?" Isaiah replies: "Here am I. Send me!" (Isaiah 6:8). You are called to a mission and wherever you happen to be, God has already given you a mission field!

If you are called to global mission and to go into the world, you need to understand that mission starts at home.

Model for mission, Acts 1:8

"But you will receive power when the Holy Spirit comes on you; and you will be my witnesses in Jerusalem and in all Judea and Samaria, and to the ends of the earth."

See the pattern? We need to be in God's will. He will equip us and first we start where we are, then move out to witness in local areas, and then see where God may send us in the world.

Sometimes the work of missionaries overseas looks more exciting than what is being done on your own doorstep! The fact is, though, that if you are a Christian you need to start in mission where God has placed you. You need to be able to support those abroad from where you are now. Start by being a missionary in your own church, home, school, college or workplace. Don't be scared, Jesus has gone on before you and prepared the way and he will never leave you – he is right at your side.

▓ Did you know?

Your church, youth group and Christian Union is a mission base. They are not there for maintenance. They do not exist to provide you a "feel-good" factor. Look at them as a battlefield hospital, a place where people come for hope, peace and healing. They are places where people have their lives turned around and then go back out to reach out and give to others.

Start by finding out information about mission. There are leaflets, magazines, books and Christian organizations that will help you. When you find a particular missionary work that fires your spirit, pass on what you have learnt and begin to support it. You can truly be a missionary right where you're standing. Check out the story below.

Born in the Ssese Islands, Enid Nazziwa went to school in Kenya, then took a YWAM discipleship course and received healthcare training. Sadly, Enid's husband had died from Aids. Back in Uganda, her father pleaded for her to come back home and help her people there, so she returned to the islands where she grew up, to apply her healthcare skills to her own people.

Enid explains: "I was by my husband's side and saw his terrible pain. I knew his death was near and from that moment I prayed a prayer in which I committed my life to those with no-one to care for them."

That's why Enid is still there today on Kitobo Island, amongst the fishermen. These men of the sea surround her as they make and repair their nets. It's evocative of a biblical scene. Enid is a woman of prayer who dedicates her life to giving basic medical care along with meeting the emotional needs of hurting people. To her community she is a bright shining light from God.

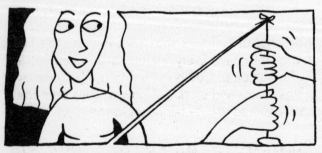

As already mentioned, to qualify to be a missionary you do not have to travel overseas. God calls many to do this, but people back home need to be informed of what's going on in the countries where missionaries have been sent. You can be an "enabler" of others. You can be a communication line for your church by reading up on what is happening and then relaying the news back to the congregation. Many missionaries abroad do not enjoy the comfort zones of home so they need to be lifted in prayer – every day! They face opposition and hostility and mockery. At the very least they miss friends and family. Don't forget they may have young children with them and face all sorts of worries to do with health and education.

Be innovative in the ways you can support your chosen mission. Be a "doer". You might want to organize a sponsored event or talk to your friends about the work that others are doing, or you might come up with a radical/crazy idea that will help the people and cause that God has put on your heart.

Global mission is like all of God's work; he inspires and achieves his goals through the thousands of believers who form the essential links of a global chain. Every link is vital and imperative to the outcome. God is in control but he gave us brains to use and work out how to overcome the obstacles that will certainly get in the way.

REMEMBER: NO CHAIN – NO GAIN!

Look on it this way: we are the builders, God the Father is the architect, God the Son is the engineer and God the Holy Spirit is the power supply. This is not mission impossible, nothing can stand in the way of God's ultimate plan for his eternal Kingdom – just feel privileged that we are chosen to help him bring it to fruition and then enter into it for eternity. Praise God that he wants us to be a part of his team.

Working together in love and showing it through practical application means charities can exist. It is amazing to think that there are Christian organizations doing awesome things, like flying hundreds of aid-carrying planes into remote and dangerous areas; these charities are made up of thousands of supporters all around the world doing their bit.

Every person has that important role to fulfil; just because you are not right on the front line you are still paramount to the mission/s being successful.

We humans are a fallen people, so we think

the glory jobs are where it's really at. Wrong. If you decide not to listen to God and go at things your own way – even if you have good intentions – the likelihood is that you will ultimately fail. God is infinite, he sees the whole picture: we are finite and only get to catch glimpses. Just trust the one who knows your destiny and you'll achieve more than you ever dreamed possible.

There are thousands of churches all over the globe made up of thousands of disciples just like you and me who in their own small way make up a mighty team that is working for the same causes. Never think your role is just a bit part. Do not ask yourself, "What can I or my little church achieve that is going to make the slightest bit of difference?" Leave these kinds of thoughts well alone – the one who is whispering these negative words to you is God's enemy, and the Devil knows that his time is short. He too has an appointment with God and believe me, you would not want to be in his shoes on Judgement Day!

You can guarantee that the particular mission that you are praying, giving and raising up is also being supported by thousands of other churches around the world. We are going to have to wait until Heaven to see all that the Church did for Jesus. But one day we will.

God needs you!

1914 was the start of the First World War, also known as the Great War. Lord Kitchener, the

War Minister in charge of the British Army, required new recruits to go to France and fight in the trenches. It was a truly horrendous war. At the time posters of Kitchener and his pointing finger were put up in public places to entice men to don a uniform and go and fight. Accompanying the picture were the words: "Your Country Needs You".

Just imagine the pointing finger of God is aimed at you. YOUR GOD NEEDS YOU! God wants his people to be well-informed; to research and digest the facts about subjects and areas that they find themselves being drawn to; and then go and tell others of what they know.

He wants us to be on the look-out, finding out what we can about the situations and people that are crying out for "disciple action" (even if they don't realize… yet!). Get involved. Encourage other young people to start taking those first steps. God is looking for disciples. He wants us to be committed to all aspects of global mission.

If you are a follower of Jesus then there's

only one option – we are his workers and his "work" will be done. But before we get going we first need to learn how to serve.

Again the perfect example is found in Jesus. Read the account of the Lord's Supper in John 13:1–17 and Luke 22:24–27. We need to serve our brothers and sisters in Christ, including those who are out there on the front line, by giving and praying, writing letters of encouragement and spreading the news about the work that they are doing. This is what God means when he tells us to GO!

Lee Jordan had the privilege of travelling with The Peace & Hope Trust to witness first-hand the work this dedicated charity does in Nicaragua, Central America.

Nicaragua in Central America is a country that geographically was in the wrong place at the wrong time. In October 1998, a tropical storm had developed into a full-blown hurricane that went by the name Mitch, a mass of cyclones that tore through all in its path. Incessant rains had flooded more than 50 rivers, knocking out bridges and roads, and 70 per cent of all crops were destroyed. Thousands were dead.

Worse was to come. On October 30 the Casita volcano erupted and mudslides claimed the lives of thousands more as whole villages disappeared. And then an earthquake hit the city of Chinandega. But parts of this land, comatosed by destruction, are now rising from the ashes. It is an Englishman who continues to sound the reveille.

Former Squadron Leader Michael Cole OBE is a human whirlwind, a 66-year-old grandfather who is continually flying across the Atlantic, stopping off in Texas to stock up on supplies for the various teams that accompany him for weeks at a time.

Mike points out: "It is essential that the team eats well in order to do a full day's work. There is no point in being ill due to lack of nutrition when the whole point of mission is to help the disadvantaged."

Nicaragua has to be visited to truly experience its diversity and indigenous people and their cultures. It lies on the Mosquito Coast (the name may describe the blood-sucking pest which is there in abundance, but the name derives from the native Miskito tribe). Nicaraguans are a mixture of English-speaking communities, people of African descent and groups such as the Miskito tribe. There is no true national identity; depending on what coast you live on you are deemed a foreigner to the other.

You will agree that Nicaragua has its difficulties. In 1990 when Nicaragua was engulfed by the wrath of nature it was a Christian man that the government of that country called on to help. Mike has an excellent track record when it comes to "getting the job done". His pioneering ventures include three unprecedented hovercraft projects in China, Nepal and Nicaragua. Communication links were set up along major rivers in these countries, so that people living in poverty in remote areas could be reached.

The Peace & Hope Trust continue to take the

message of Jesus Christ to a hurting and desperate country. Mild earthquakes (shakes) are part of the daily experience in Nicaragua. At present missionaries (long- and short-term, old and young) are constructing an earthquake-proof house made with straw bales that will double as an ever-present example to follow and the headquarters for the trust in the capital of Managua.

Mike says: "Nicaraguans are the key to the renewing of their country." There are many people that the trust has given a lifeline to. But as Mike has already said, it's the people who have to learn from the missionaries. The teams are made up of all kinds of people from young and old and from different countries, skilled and non-skilled. Again it is that chain formation, and every link is vital to the success of each mission.

Like other charities The Peace & Hope Trust only exists because of its supporters back home, who are praying, financially giving and going into their schools with updates, then into wider communities and even going as long- and short-term missionaries to Nicaragua.

It is true that in Mike Cole, God has chosen an organizational genius, but Nicaragua will not get anywhere without God's foot soldiers. Whoever you are, your role is important and instrumental. God has equipped us with a variety of gifts, both natural and spiritual and Mike Cole's favourite Bible verse is: "From everyone who has been given much, much will be demanded; and from the one who has been entrusted with much, much more will be asked" (Luke 12:48).

As I witnessed Mike and his team constructing

an extension to the school that the trust had built some years before, I saw all of those various God-given gifts coming together through hard graft and a good sense of humour. These were modern-day disciples expressing God's love to an impoverished people. It was demonstrated in two ways, practical application and the respect and heart-felt feelings that the team members had for the people of Nicaragua.

And, of course, many countries that missionaries travel to have other dangers. Nicaragua is no exception. It is where Colombian drug smugglers choose to distribute their illegal goods. One village we visited is suspected of helping collect drugs from the river that meanders past their wooden shacks. Apparently the drug smugglers throw parcels overboard at the mouth of the river, which flows into the Caribbean, and the packages float down to the awaiting villagers.

Without Mike's influence and the respect that he has, the village would otherwise be a dangerous location for well-meaning Christians. But since when have Jesus' people stayed away from danger?

Whoever thinks that Christians are timid and using faith as a crutch need their heads examined. Being a missionary may mean going into a war-torn country or a part of the world where famine is rife, or where Christians are not welcomed. Many missionaries face hardship and even death. Going for God should be seen as a privilege. Only God can change the world, and one day he will, but we can do our bit now and have a life-changing effect on individuals and communities. God asks us to go into the world with the message of the Cross and if we confess to be his disciples for the 21st century then we have to do what other Christians did in the 1st century: we have to go and tell the world the Good News and demonstrate it in our very lives.

When you get to Heaven

Oswald Smith travelled around communicating the message of the Great Commission (Matthew 28:16–20) and told a story called *Will you be lonely in Heaven?*

He would tell the story of a man named John Chinaman, representing those in foreign lands who came to Christ through the work of Christian missionaries. In this story, John Chinaman was asked what he would do when he got to Heaven. He said: "Firstly, when I get to Heaven, I am going to walk the golden pavements until I find Jesus, the one who saved me. Then I will fall down and worship him. Then, I will continue to walk the streets of Heaven until I find a missionary who came to my country with the Christian message. I will grasp his hand and thank him for his part in my salvation.

"Thirdly, I will search the streets of Heaven until I find the men, women, the young people and the children who prayed and gave money to make it possible for that missionary to come. I will grasp their hands and thank them for the part they played in my salvation."

Oswald Smith concludes the story with a challenge. "My friend, will there be any John

"I WANNA GO DEEPER BUT I DON'T KNOW HOW TO RUN... "

Above is a line from the song "Deeper" by the Christian rock band Delirious? and the words are so true. God will give us the desire to forge a deeper relationship with him but we must always seek him first to find out how we are to go about his particular plan for us. If we don't look to God initially then we will not be able to walk, let alone run!

Delirious? are on a mission to take Jesus to the world through their music. Anyone who has seen them play will know that worship Delirious? style proves that Jesus is relevant to the 21st century. It's powerful, uplifting and a blast in the face of the cynical music world. Delirious? pack a godly punch!

Bands like Delirious? paved the way for other Christian acts that are now reaching out for their generation. The missionary field is a vast one and includes all types of people and professions. There are musicians like the Tribe who believe in sharing the Gospel where they live in the city of Manchester. Just think of the teachers who choose to teach in the inner-cities. These qualified men and women could just as easily choose an area where there isn't much trouble and the financial rewards are greater. Missionaries should be everywhere.

Plane survival

A unique Floatplane service provides a lifeline to those who live on the Ssese Islands on Lake Victoria. Around 150,000 people live on these islands and they rely on this innovative transport.

Without it, the main route to these islands is via an unreliable ferry service connecting the largest island to the mainland. Apart from that, canoes (a handful with motors and canopies) are the sole transport between and beyond these islands.

One pilot commented on the lake being more like the sea, and that in a boat you may encounter huge swells, rough seas, tropical storms, torrential rain, high winds and waterspouts, leaving your boat filling up with water. There are no lifejackets, no flares and no lifeboats. That's why every year so many who travel on water perish. Imagine if the charity's team of pilots, engineers and other team members had decided not to go!

Chinaman from any country in the world who will come and thank you when you get to Heaven, or will you be lonely in Heaven? Will no-one recognize you except a few of your relatives and friends?"

Could there be any greater joy in your heart when you are in Heaven than to have multitudes of people, from every nation, stopping you every now and again to say that they are in eternity because of the people who prayed, gave, chose to go and do.

Never think that there is anything wrong with imagining what Heaven will be like. We should be looking ahead to eternity – we are assured of it. Forget floating around on fluffy clouds and competing with angels in the harp choir. Heaven will be beyond our wildest dreams and nothing like the cartoons we often see. It's ironic because the painters and sketchers of this unbiblical Heaven don't even know Jesus.

There's nothing wrong with reflecting on what God has promised his believers. Jesus told the disciples in John 14:2–4 "In my Father's house are many rooms; if it were not so, I would have told you. I am going there to prepare a place for you. And if I go and prepare a place for you, I will come back and take you to be with me that you also may be where I am. You know the way to the place where I am going."

Jesus is the way. He also told us: "Do not store up for yourselves treasures on earth, where moth and rust destroy, and where thieves break in and steal. But store up for yourselves treasures in heaven, where moth and rust do not destroy, and where thieves do not break in and steal. For where your treasure is, there your heart will be also" (Matthew 6:19–21).

Jesus left to us the blueprint to follow: he tells us that our hearts, minds and very thoughts should be focused on the hope and our guaranteed future in Heaven. If we take Jesus at his word, then his encouragement will get us through any difficult times or desperate situations. There really is a joy set before us. Jesus went on ahead of us to prepare for our arrival and he will reward his workers.

So do not think Heaven is something we cannot grasp. When we get to paradise there will be work to do and an eternal purpose. We will truly praise Jesus in all that we do. Worshipping the King of eternity will be a reality that we will never tire of because it will not be like a never-ending church service; it will encompass everything we do, from working, to exalting, to living.

We will be given a new body – one fit for the people of God and for a life that will go on forever. But we must not fall into the trap of thinking, "Oh well, there's not much point in doing anything now, I'll wait until Heaven." Our future and position in eternity will be determined by what we do on earth – ask yourself, are you truly walking in God's ways? If you are then start taking bigger steps forward, but if you are not, then for your future's sake get going – there is always time to get right with God while you are still breathing, but do not delay: there's a job to be done – by... you!

A wonderful verse that has encouraged Christians for the last 2,000 years is found in Hebrews 12:2, "Let us fix our eyes on Jesus, the author and perfecter of our faith, who for the joy set before him endured the cross, scorning its shame, and sat down at the right hand of the throne of God."

Eternal perspective

Modern society is fast, scary and constantly "in ya face": a stressful time in the earth's history. Technology has advanced at such a rate that nature is affected. Unless you live out in the sticks, away from a built-up town or city then you probably haven't experienced a real night sky. Artificial lights and the 24-hour work ethos have not only given the earth a different look physically, but also changed the patterns and natural lifestyles of millions of people.

I wonder if nature is crying out for more peaceful times, where day was day and night was night? When the dawn signalled a new day it meant hustle and bustle but when night fell there would be a stillness and time of calm. This is no longer the case; trying to have a quiet time and finding a place for peaceful meditation on God's Word is no easy thing in a 24–7 society.

The apostle Paul says in Romans 8:19–21: "The creation waits in eager expectation for the sons of God to be revealed. For the creation was subjected to frustration, not by its own choice, but by the will of the one who subjected it, in hope that the creation itself will be liberated from its bondage to decay and brought into the glorious freedom of the children of God."

In Genesis we read that sin is the cause of nature's troubles, but the world by and large doesn't see it that way and man thinks that because of all the scientific and industrial advances, he is in charge. Sadly the environment tells a different story and it seems the more we apparently progress the worse it gets.

All of creation is groaning under the weight of the demands of the modern world: peace is hard to find. But do not despair: Heaven awaits us. Take a moment and ask God to reveal this truth; read your Bibles and search out the verses that describe Heaven, and remember that we are just a dot in the timescale of eternity. This world in its current form will not last for ever but a new Heaven and earth will be ours to enjoy: the way God always wanted us to! But before we get there we have to get going with the mission of spreading

God's holy Word. It's not easy, but there are others that are just waiting to hear the Good News and when they do they will respond just like you and I did. Being a link in God's chains means we do not always see the results of our labour, but one day we will and what a day that will be. God's plan is rolling on and going onwards is part of ours. The Bible says that soon God will wrap history up and create a new wonderful world. But before he does, let's get out there and "go" for it!

On my first mission to Ethiopia in 1994, I can remember quite clearly being prepared, but not as prepared as I should have been. I can remember getting off the aeroplane and being engulfed by the heat, the smell of the city and seeing such a beautiful array of people. I recall all the emotions, even now, of the time we drove through the centre of Addis Ababa, the capital of that country.

If I close my eyes it is as if I am still sitting in the car. I remember looking out on to the streets to my left, seeing half-naked people running around, begging. I witnessed children forced into prostitution because of the poverty, and seeing illegal drug distribution as if it was just a daily event: sadly that is exactly what it is.

What a contrast when I turned my attention to the other side of the street. Talk about the "haves and have-nots". In London we do have rich areas and just around the corner working-class communities, but the Addis Ababa divide was so apparent. To my Western mind I asked why this great poverty line was symbolized by the street? One word summed it all up – greed. The wealthy used the poor people in order to gain even more. The poor barely survive. It is indicative of the Third World: the rich citizens that make up these countries do not distribute financial gain and aid from abroad fairly or wisely: they claim virtually all of it for themselves.

This is why it is imperative to support "Fair Trade" initiatives and to buy produce like carpets, coffee, tea and sports gear that are endorsed by the Fair Trade watchdog. This really is something we can quite easily apply ourselves to; it only takes a little bit of awareness when we are out shopping. We really have no excuse. Maybe next time when we are out shopping we should think of the poor and suffering people of the world and it should prick our conscience into simple action.

You see, yet again, we can be active without necessarily being on the front line. When I experienced the poor of Addis Ababa, a compassion welled up inside of me, through tears of grief and indignation I was brought to the point of wanting to do all that I could to help.

So *What4* started to get stuck in. We joined in with a centre that was supporting prostitutes as they went through rehabilitation, and helped to construct a runway in a remote part of Ethiopia so that aircraft could fly in much needed medical aid and personnel. We had the privilege of assisting to build a clinic at the side of the runway – the only clinic in an 80-mile radius where something like 56,000 people do not have access to any medical facilities! Can you imagine a similar situation in Europe, or in the USA? It seems to go unnoticed in many far-away countries.

Since when has a small land been insignificant to God? Who would have thought that a tiny country like Israel would have been the place where God would choose a people where the Saviour of the World would be one of them? Israel is the place where Jesus will return to and it is rarely out of the news. It only consists of 6 million people but the very name causes stirring in the hearts of all the nations.

The Christians in Ethiopia had a major impact on me. When I first visited I went with the mindset that I was the one who would offer my skills and gifts, but I learnt very quickly that they had/have so much to offer and to give me. It is extremely humbling and proves that belonging to God's team is a two-way process. As is being a missionary. You allow others to impact you as you impact others.

In Ethiopia we climbed high into the mountains and surveyed the panoramic splendour. God's creation is awesome. Hundreds of miles of mountains full of trees – their green leaves were so vivid. We truly serve a magnificent God.

After our heavenly experience we came back down to earth with a bump. Driving through the city's suburbs we approached the British Embassy. Again, frustration welled up within me, as I saw this Buckingham Palace-like building standing in a land of poverty. Where families of fourteen live in one-room shacks that contain one bed, where every family member gets to sleep in it once every fortnight. But, across the road on the "sunny" side of the street members of the British Embassy have their own Tesco, their own mini-shopping precinct, their own swimming pool and golf course. Of course, everything is self-contained.

Yet, the irony is that these two diverse cultures have something in common – they both need to hear Good News of Jesus Christ!

Going to another country and experiencing a different way of life has an immediate impact: it momentarily changes your life and hopefully should for evermore. The world becomes a whole new ball game. I have a longing to gather up as many young people as possible and take them to an entirely different culture, expose them to another way of life, and for them then to give something of true worth to the people they come across. But the cold fact is: if we cannot give to less-privileged people in our own country, or where God has placed us, then there is little hope that we will be able to do the same overseas. Just because certain countries on planet earth sound exotic it might be tempting to imagine that God has called us to go there, but if he hasn't then we are outside of his plan for us – not a good idea! But he promises that if we seek him we shall find his purpose and our destiny. If you trust in Jesus then God does have a definite plan for your life!

OBEYING THE CALL

Stuart King is a former missionary who advises that a wanna-be missionary needs to have a passion for the lost in his or her own community/country before taking the message to the rest of the world. So start local and then go global.

Over 50 years ago Stuart was serving with the Royal Air Force (RAF). He had survived the

Second World War and looked forward to the security and challenge of a rewarding career. Yet, he knew that God was calling him to a faraway land – the dangerous and impossible conditions of the Sudan, in north-east Africa, the largest country of that continent. A land that was steeped in history; in the previous century the British military had known heavy loss and the glory of victory. In the capital, Khartoum, the great Victorian Army officer, General Gordon, lost his life as the British Army fought against the Mahdists; another famous leader of men, Lord Kitchener, later reclaimed Khartoum. So for the young Stuart King it was a country that had known upheaval and tragedy.

A land made up of Muslims in the north and mainly Christians in the south, apart from local tribes who are animists (a belief that material objects like rocks are alive) and do not adhere to either of the two established religions in that country. Even today a war of oppression by the Khartoum Government is being fought against the separatists in the south. When God calls you to a place like the Sudan, you have to be certain that he is the one doing the calling.

For Stuart it meant the start of an exciting new life: one in which he would survive a plane crash and meet his future wife. Stuart King is a man who always seeks God's counsel before embarking on any spiritual journey. We would be well-advised to heed his advice: before going we need to seek God's will.

Note how Stuart answers the following questions, put to him by some young people of *What4*.

Why Africa and how did you know that it was God's will?

"Well I had been praying for months. There were other alternatives: staying in the Air Force or going into aircraft design and research. As I was praying though, and reading my Bible, I was struck by the incredible faith of Abraham. I mean the famous 'hall of fame' in Hebrews 11 (readers: take a look, it's a must read). Abraham went out not knowing where he was going! I could relate. I didn't know what the future of Africa held for me yet. I knew that God was saying to me very clearly these words: 'Although you don't know where you are going, I'm calling you to go out and to trust in me.'"

How did you handle the idea of going to the Sudan? You must have been afraid?

"In Sudan, especially in the South, the people live a very basic lifestyle, but I didn't have too many problems adjusting. This was God's call and it was a privilege. There was excitement in following God's call, and to be where I was supposed to be! When God calls you, he helps you to adjust. That was my wife's experience in Sudan as well. I met her out there and we were later married. As for fears and concerns, I wasn't afraid of what I would be facing but I was sad at the thought of what I was leaving. I was very enamoured with aviation, and particularly with aircraft research and design. It was quite a wrench in that way, to say goodbye to that by going out to Africa."

When you sprang this "going to Africa business" on friends and family, were they supportive?

"I think my father was quite disappointed that I did not stay in the Air Force or go into an aeronautics design career. My mother, an ardent supporter of missions, however, was quietly very supportive. Other people whom I knew, Christians included, were not so supportive. Some of them questioned the whole concept of my plan to build an aviation outreach charity at that stage. It was such a new idea that quite a lot of them thought it was a bit of a South Sea bubble that would pop and become a wild goose chase. Some of them almost laughed at the thought! So there were mixed reactions, but through it all was a case of knowing that God was calling, whatever other people felt. And there was, of course, prayer support from people who shared my vision of an aviation fellowship, embryonic though it was at that stage."

What advice would you give to someone who felt that God was telling them to go?

"Be totally willing to obey God. That means being willing to go, and equally to be willing not to go. Once we are willing, it's my experience that God will speak and show his will much more clearly and plainly. Then take time to confirm by prayer and by reading your Bible to hear carefully what God is saying to you. It is important to know God has called you, because when things get rough later, you need to have that assurance."

Stuart King went on to build Mission Aviation Fellowship; today MAF is an international charity and a vital lifeline for people living in remote areas of the world.

A young Stuart King listened to God and in faith and trust obeyed his call to go. So if anyone reading this book thinks that their name is being called to follow God at home or overseas then take time to pray and study the Word. Make sure that you know his purpose for you. Be prepared for hard times, but like Stuart says, be assured that this is his will for you. If it is, you will know! God's plans will be accomplished but don't miss out on the role that he has for you.

Stephen Montgomery took a year out to give time to God and go to Uganda to help work on the IT services of a Christian charity. Read on to see what he learned during his time there.

I was thinking about all my wonderful attributes whilst completing my UCAS personal statement and mulling over what I wanted to do in the year that I had decided to take out. I'd been to Africa a couple of times and got hooked on the country, so I wanted to go back and do something worthwhile. I knew that I didn't want to spend a whole twelve months abroad as I wanted to have a few months to do other things as well.

I wrote off to various mission organizations, but didn't really find anything that grabbed me. It would have been so easy to go for second best or just to give up. I had already considered it at least once but I knew this was something that God wanted me to do, so I pressed on.

In a *What4* mailing there was a little box asking readers to pray for someone to go to Uganda for eight months to fill the position in the IT department of a charity operation over there. Well, I did pray, because I'm a technical kind of person and that sort of thing grabs me. I never thought that I would be the person to fulfil the role. I did think that it would be a nice thing to do and it got to the stage where I thought it would be worth a try – trying proved to be almost as difficult as some of the things I did out in Uganda!

It wasn't until over six months later (and quite a few metaphorical mountains had to be climbed) that I got an official yes. It was during a camping trip that I received the phone call confirming that my ticket was booked. Less than a week later, I flew out to Uganda, not knowing exactly when I would return to England; neither had I been briefed on what my exact role would be.

Of course, I was aware that it would involve IT but beyond that I didn't have a clue. However, God had a plan and knew the date of my return. The biggest thing that I learnt as I stepped out in faith was that whilst I was in Uganda, I had to trust him to look after every single part of my life.

The scope of the work was diverse. My main tasks were to administrate, troubleshoot and upgrade the charity's e-mail services for 150 missionaries, organizations and church workers spread across Uganda. The server was on its last legs, and the job would have given a computer whiz a run for their money! I think God must have studied hard, because he was able to help me learn all about the crazy workings of Microsoft, such as DHCP server, IP routing and other techno things that I didn't even think existed in England, let alone a Third World country. Many times I turned to God for help.

Living in Kampala, the capital city, was a challenge of its own. Nothing seems to work and when you call the phone/electricity/water board to report a fault, you get told that they are not working today! By the end of the week, when you finally get them to come, they end up tearing your building to pieces, only to decide that they can't do anything now as they need a part that they cannot get until next week!

I attended a fast-growing home church full of other missionary families, where I really felt at home. I was extremely blessed to be provided with my own house for some of the stay, as well as a mobile phone and a car, which I didn't use much – public transport was far too exciting!

Families were always inviting me to their homes for meals, games or to watch a movie. I was even put up for the night when I locked myself out of the house – accidentally, I assure you!

The local Pentecostal church which I attended a number of times had seven services on a Sunday morning! In each service there were over 1,000 worshippers. I forged good friendships with the youth there despite their tending to whisper when conducting one-on-one conversations (fortunately in English, although the main languages are Lugandan and Kiswahili). Because of my newly found friendships, I spent a lot of time getting out into the "real" Kampala. I also got involved in construction, visiting orphanages, and helped to set up the projection equipment in various villages so the *Jesus Film* could be shown and I participated at the Friday night youth events.

One thing struck me as I lived among the Ugandan people and that was that they know how to live life to the full, even though they possess, materially, so much less than we do. Gradually, Uganda began to affect me.

Upon reflection I realized that after coping with so many people and having had to adapt to such a range of personalities, I have developed the spiritual fruit of patience. Ugandans are a laid-back people and it takes a while to grow accustomed to this. They are so mellow that it took a policeman half-an-hour to arrest me for driving the wrong way down a one-way street. I will just say that it wasn't marked in any way so it could not have been my fault. However, I did manage to persuade him of my innocence and he let me go. But in truth it was a scary situation. And it wasn't the only one...

A small but nasty black mamba snake had decided that my kitchen sink was its home. Many toads also preferred the concrete of the floor to a murky bed of a pond. Some nights we heard shooting – once close enough for people to think that it was in our compound. On that particular night I stood by ready to dive under my covers. There was also a potentially life-threatening virus epidemic called Ebola, which killed hundreds of people. It was rife but thankfully it never reached Kampala, but if it had, it would probably have been too late for the missionaries, because at the time the surrounding countries were not allowing anyone access across their borders. But even in the turmoil of all these situations, I developed a stronger faith in the fact that God was my protector.

Oh and by the way, be thankful for our electoral system; compared to Uganda's it's streets upon streets ahead. It was General Election time while I was there – Ugandan style! It consisted of candidates all claiming that their particular party had the best manifesto. The funny thing was they never got round to explaining what it was. Loyal supporters of candidates would frequently take it out on voters on the other side. Okay, it sounds like the House of Commons but our corridors of power are in a different – and much fairer – league.

Opposing views over there means continual

shouting, rioting, deaths and vandalism. One night there was even some bombings; fortunately no one was killed but the headlines read that bombs had "rocked" the city centre!

Apart from these sometimes precarious circumstances I generally stayed in good health. My only problems were mango flies. You are supposed to iron all your clothes to kill the pest's eggs – otherwise they will hatch larvae and the flies will burrow under your skin. If this happens then Vaseline and squeezing hard helps! However, on my return to the UK, I discovered that I was turning a shade of yellow and eventually ended up in a specialist medical centre in London for a week while many tests were carried out. The results were inconclusive and doctors never did find out which disease caused what, but I know that God healed me from a combination of glandular fever, Bilharzia, Hepatitis F and a viral infection.

I had been warned about the effect of "reverse culture shock", and had experienced it before. However, it wasn't the massive contrast of England and Uganda that got me, maybe because I had been prepared for it; what gripped me was the difference between the England I now saw and the England that I had left behind months before. Even now, I know that I still have to trust God for everything! If anything my Ugandan mission has deepened my dependency on him.

"Now strengthen my hands!"

"Our God lives and speaks!" These were the carefully chosen words of Bernard Terlouw, who

IF YOU DON'T TRUST IN GOD THEN IT WILL BE MISSION IMPOSSIBLE.

leads a missionary team in Kenya. They sum up the traumatic but life-changing events that took place during one unforgettable summer. Here is Bernard's account, followed by the testimonies of the two individuals through whom God chose to bring about his purposes and blessings during that time.

One Friday about 9am, three armed robbers assaulted my wife Margriet and her Swiss missionary friend, Doris, in our kitchen in Nairobi. They had broken into the kitchen, grabbed my wife and Doris and pointed pistols to their heads. Margriet later described her feelings at the time of the attack in an e-mail to friends. She wrote:

Can you imagine – a gun aimed at your head! I suppose you cannot. Until then, a pistol was only something you see in a movie. But that thought has dramatically changed. I can hardly describe what came into my mind at those moments. I was terribly afraid and shocked and the first thing I thought was: "My kids! I can't die now, I want to take care of them, they need me!" And I prayed: "Oh Lord – help us!"

The men tried to drag Margriet and Doris into

a large cupboard, but with boldness both women resisted and broke free. They caught Doris and began to beat her, but Doris screamed: "Go away, in Jesus' name!" This appeared to stun the intruders. It was enough time for Margriet to attempt to break free. With her heart thumping and knowing that she had only one chance she bolted for the door. Praise God that she managed to escape. She had no time to think. All she knew was she had to reach her car and alert the authorities. She managed to reach some neighbours – staff of the British Embassy – the guard there immediately called in the mobile team of security officers, who responded at lightning speed.

Meanwhile back at our home, the robbers had been so frightened because of Doris's continual prayer: "Go away in Jesus' name," that they fled from the building! It had been a horrible experience but Jesus had been in the midst of the fear.

After the alarm was sounded, our compound was buzzing with security guards. But though the perpetrators had left their evil presence and it seemed to stain the very atmosphere, this was our home!

During the assault, all our neighbours on the same compound had been in their houses. Only when the security guard piled on to the compound did they realize a dangerous incident had occurred. Yet, we thank God that he kept Margriet and Doris safe. He was there before the security guards, and he was present during the attack. We were reminded of the power that is in the name of Jesus. The robbers panicked because of the powerful presence of the Lord!

It was only days later when we realized the full impact of this terrible experience. We remained frightened and vulnerable. I could hardly bring myself to leave Margriet alone, and when she had to go out, she hardly dared to cross a street. Groups of men to her represented the robbers and she felt continually threatened and the memories of the assault were re-lived.

But the Lord showed his love and care again. One night, our friend and colleague Andy Medlicott visited us. He said that he had been praying and that the Lord had put us in his heart. Andy knew that he had to come and read a passage from the Bible. The verse was Nehemiah 6:9:

"They were all trying to frighten us,
thinking, 'Their hands will get too weak for
   the work,
and it will not be completed.'
But I prayed, 'Now strengthen my hands.'"

That was an enormous encouragement! This was the word of the Lord for us! And we realized the perspective: do not get discouraged and do not let it stop your work. Together with Andy we prayed: "Please Lord, strengthen our hands."

The words were so right and perfect for our situation and the encouragement that we really needed, for that very week I had to journey to Uganda and it meant leaving Margriet and the children behind in Nairobi.

When I said goodbye to my wife at the

airport and when I arrived at Entebbe, all the time I was wishing that I was with my family in our home. I had to pull myself together!

Again God's Word was the answer. I drew great encouragement from Nehemiah, the passage that God had told Andy to bring to my family.

On the day I arrived, I had to drive for the first time to an aircraft hangar at Kajjansi, totally unaware of what I would find there. As I entered the hangar I stopped dead in my tracks. I was perplexed and overcome in amazement. My eyes filled with tears as I read the words that someone had painted on the wall in large letters:

> "They were all trying to frighten us,
>   thinking, 'Their hands will get too weak for
>   the work,
> and it will not be completed.'
> But I prayed, 'Now strengthen my hands.'"

In one incredible moment, it felt like all the tension just evaporated and the peace I needed from God flooded through me, filling my soul. It was not until later that I found out who had painted these words, but in that one moment I knew why God had put them there. Praise him!

This was "electrifying" encouragement in the fact that our God is a sovereign Lord. He knows exactly what everyone of us is going through. He wants to speak into our hearts and bring us closer to him. The knowledge that evil really exists is a frightening reality, as is the knowledge that the enemy will use it against us. My family and friend came face to face with it; the feeling of fear has not disappeared... yet! But just like Nehemiah, each one of us can pray and then carry out the work we must do for him. In his power only – and by no other way – it will be completed.

Glory to Jesus.

Isn't it amazing that God's purpose works through a providential chain? Just look how Bernard and his wife drew comfort from God's Word. Look how God used their friend Andy to begin the process of mental healing and then how the same words on the hangar wall strengthened Bernard when he was separated from Margriet and the children. God is always only a breath away.

The words on the wall of the Kajjansi hangar were painted there because of a request from Geoff Hillier to a young missionary, an aircraft maintenance engineer based in Uganda. This scripture in Nehemiah had also been an encouragement to Geoff during his training, and had helped increase his faith and enabled him to press on further towards his goal of being a missionary worker overseas.

Geoff had no idea how God would use the Bible verse in Nehemiah in the future but we must never forget that God is outside of our timescale. He exists in dimensions that are beyond our comprehension. He transcends all earthly thoughts, creations, inventions, ideas, human brilliance and anything else sceptics try to come up with to disprove him. Quite simply he is… God! Bernard and Geoff know this for a fact. But it's great to hear accounts of Christians who trust in God for their future. Geoff explains:

The reason I chose this verse dates back to when I was in the Royal Airforce and considering leaving it to work for God overseas. I was taking a particularly tricky course in repairing aircraft structure and was struggling to keep up! I remember thinking, "Well, If I can't get through this then I won't be much use to God working on aircraft that would be carrying vital aid and equipment to needy people." He brought to my mind the Nehemiah scripture that at the time I had been studying; it encouraged me so much.

The fact that God cared about the blister-inducing, knuckle-grazing, callous developing works of Nehemiah's hands, and indeed mine, blew me away! He was able to bring strength and skill to the hands that had a will to serve him. Even in the practical work of charities, God is there encouraging and enabling. NO matter what God calls us to, Nehemiah is proof that God will supply all you need to do the job. And don't listen to negative thoughts such as: "Oh I'm no good at… " (You don't need to be Einstein to fill in the gaps!). It just doesn't wash with our God. He is the Creator of all – everything! He is certainly qualified to help you acquire the skills that you need.

Happily I went on to pass the course with flying colours. Now here I am working in Africa!

For a *What4* mission team member who visited Uganda, the Nehemiah scripture that Geoff Hillier asked her to paint on the Kajjansi hangar wall certainly left its mark on her life! Stephanie recalls:

It was about this point during the mission that the Bible studies, which I had wanted to be doing everyday – from first thing in the morning – actually started happening! And this scripture from Nehemiah 6 was such a beautiful blessing. I don't recall ever coming across it before but it certainly had the best opportunity for sinking its way into my head. It really isn't often that you spend more than a day deliberating over every letter of every word, never mind the arrangement! It is amazing – the amount of resources that God takes a hold of and uses to encourage his children. Beautiful!

Nothing is too hard for our God. What is impossible with man, is possible with God – Jesus said it, so it must be true. Just imagine if Geoff had not taken any notice of the message and scripture that God had put in his heart. If he had listened to his own thoughts, he would never have travelled overseas, which would have meant that he would never have written God's words on the hangar wall. Think of the repercussions for Bernard's family. Poor old Bernard would have been so discouraged when he first arrived in Uganda, that his own work for God may have come to nothing. And Stephanie would never have been touched in such an in-depth way.

Praise God that he has a plan and can see the whole picture. He is infinite, we are finite. Thankfully it is not we who are in charge. We are his soldiers; some of us achieve higher ranks in God's army but we all have a job to do and if we trust in our God we will succeed!

GOD'S PEOPLE ARE ON A MISSION

Never assume that being a missionary means moving home to live somewhere else, permanently. As the words in capitals above state, God wants us for his short-term and long-term will. Sharon Francis obeyed God's temporary call when she was a teenager:

I went on a short-term mission with *What4* in August 2000. I chose to go on a short-term mission because I have a heart for working with street children and orphans, and it seemed a good starting point. Here's a summary of what I did in Uganda and what I learned.

I was part of a team of 25 who embarked on a nine-hour flight. We stayed at the Red Chilli Hideaway: it was basic accommodation with bunk beds, toilets, showers and excellent food. It was quite Western in style, which made it a good relaxing place to come back to at the end of a hard day's work.

We worked with two churches: Nakawa Baptist Church and Kampala Pentecostal Church (KPC). Nakawa Baptist Church is situated in a very poor village with high unemployment. At Nakawa we did some building work for the church; visiting families living in one-room houses shared with up to fifteen people! We met with the children of the village and gave them balloons, games, skipping ropes, colouring books, crayons, balls and bubbles; we also did some Bible teaching.

The mission enabled the team to work alongside an organization called Compassion International (CI) which supports individual children through a sponsorship programme. This pays for any medical aid and for children to go to school. We helped CI to set up a library for the children to use.

KPC is a richer church, working with people in the centre of Kampala. It has four services on a Sunday; about 2,000 worshippers attend each one. Ten of the team, including me, joined KPC's youth team, City Lights; we went into three schools, a remand home for teenagers, a children's home and a hospital.

The children's home was an excellent experience. It has 17 individual houses with eight children living in each home with a "mama" (a kind of foster mum). They live as a normal family and the children are all so happy, and the mamas are full of love for them. The children are victims of homelessness and find themselves alone and on the streets; some are parentless because of the legacy from the Ugandan Civil War, and some because of the Aids virus. We were able to spend time with the families, playing with the children and helping with the hand-washing and with the dishes.

I had an excellent time in Uganda and I feel it has changed me forever. It has shown me how much I need God in my life and that I can't manage without him. It puts things into perspective as well; you learn to appreciate more what you have in life.

I would definitely recommend going on a mission like this to everyone. But be warned... It will change you forever!

The words in the box overleaf are traditionally known as the Great Commission and modern-day believers have often neglected them. Today the challenge still is to reach the peoples of every nation and tongue with the Good News about Jesus: in fact the need to carry out the Great Commission is greater now than at any other stage in the history of the Church! Sometimes, however, we find ourselves less committed and less

Remember a missionary is a Christian who demonstrates a global attitude, but applies it locally. **What4** has a host of projects that will allow you to go into the UK and to travel overseas. For details see the Appendix at the end of this book.

Jesus clearly commanded his Church to give itself... without reservation! You are a part of the Church and have a mission to take the Gospel to the far ends of the earth.

The Great Commission (Matthew 28:18-20)

Then Jesus came to them and said: "All authority in heaven and on earth has been given to me. Therefore go and make disciples of all nations, baptising them in the name of the Father and of the Son and of the Holy Spirit, and teaching them to obey everything I have commanded you. And surely I am with you always, to very end of the age."

convinced of the priorities of world mission than ever before. We need to return to the words of Jesus and obey them with a fresh desire and commitment.

⠿ Major fact coming up

Do you know that the Bible is a book about a mission? It is God's mission of rescuing the human race, God's mission for mobilizing his people to communicate Good News. From cover to cover, it is a manual to help us live a life that is on mission. Read it, develop a passion for God's Word, get to know its characters and their situations and challenges, get to know its Author – God – and allow the Holy Spirit to speak to you through the supernatural words that are the Bible.

To recap and six reasons why 21st-century disciples should GO!

1. It will help you to play your part in the Big Picture of what God is doing in the world.
2. Jesus commanded his disciples to go.
3. It will help you to become involved in the wonderful process of bringing hope to people who live in difficult circumstances.
4. It will help you to be practical about your faith.
5. It will allow you to be impacted by a different culture, which will broaden your horizons, and you will gain a new heart for the lost.
6. Your life and world will be changed in a very real sense.

Chapter 4

Do

Q What For?

A *Disciples should be practising spiritual DIY.*

Ever stopped to wonder?

Have you ever stopped for a moment and thought about how many people in an average week, or even during the course of a day, are doing things to help us? For instance, preparing food for us, being friends to us, loving us, helping us in many different ways. I imagine that you will be surprised when you think about the people that you meet every week, those you don't even know who are doing things to help you. Just think of your school or college, or your home and family environment, or even those that

Do you "Do It Yourself"? Or are you likely to let someone else do the doing? We all have the ability to make a difference to those around us, through our actions and words. The act of doing is always a personal decision but when we take action (however small) our doing changes the world.

Jesus told the parable of the sheep and the goats as an example of the difference that our "doing" really makes to God and to our destinies in eternity. (Read Matthew's Gospel, 25:31–46. See Jesus' reply to the righteous in verse 40 and his reply to the unrighteous in verse 45.)

Make a decision today to be a "doer" for God!

work in your community who are doing things to enable others to have a better quality of life.

Just the simple things that we take for granted in the comfortable West are only a dream in the Third World: like refuse collection and road sweepers. Millions of people around the globe have to live surrounded by filth and squalor because no one collects their rubbish – it just rots in their street, where rats and disease join together just to add to the misery. There are many other services we could add to the list: the emergency services, doctors, hospital staff, child supervisors and care organizations. I could go on.

The cynic might reply with something like this: "So what, do they want medals? It's their job, they get paid for doing it." True they do but just imagine our country existing without these people. It's a scary thought. All these people form a giant body that helps our society to enjoy all of its benefits; compared to the suffering people of the world we live in an utter abundance of luxury. We've never had it so good. Because other people go out and do, we benefit.

As disciples of Jesus we should be at the forefront when it comes to doing. Jesus commands us to visit the sick, go into the prisons, to love the unloved and to tell the world of his truth. Christians are supposed to "do". We can only do by doing. So let's go and do. Jesus has done the hard work of laying the foundation and continues to do the building, now he wants us to do our part. Jesus is the Master Carpenter but we should be seriously into spiritual DIY.

There's a kingdom to build and many more workers need to hear the message. We don't know who they are but God does. He has known them since before the world was made (Ephesians 1:4). If we decide to get doing then the quicker others will come and their thirst for answers will be quenched. They are waiting for us. In their hearts they know they belong to something. Deep inside they have a longing but they will not know what that longing is until one of us tells them. There is so much to do for our future brothers and sisters; we must do for them what others have done for us. Do have faith – God's will be done – but first we have to do his will.

Streetwise

John Hughes is a young man who believes the only way to serve Jesus is by preparing to be radical. He believes Christians should not be "ashamed of their faith" and he backs up this brave thought by doing what he preaches.

John is an intelligent person who has a passion to talk to people about Jesus. Five years ago he "re-committed" his life to Christ after being involved in a Christian cult and wasn't certain if he had truly given his life to Jesus as a young boy when he used to go to regular Sunday school.

For John the re-commitment was serious, there were no doubts: he accepted Jesus Christ wholeheartedly. There was no going back. At the time he was living in London and had an important job. He worshipped at Westminster Chapel under the well-known preacher R.T. Kendal. It was "RT" who introduced him to an evangelistic outreach called Pilot Lights, where Christians from all over London would go into the streets of the capital handing out Christian literature and asking the question: "If you die tonight would you be sure that you would go to Heaven?", a question that guarantees an immediate response and it is a good conversational opener.

John moved to Kent two years ago but continues to witness to people in the city when he has any free time. But he is more likely to be seen on the streets of his local town handing out Bible tracts and striking up conversations with shoppers, high-street workers and anyone else he meets – to John these people represent the lost that Jesus died for.

There is nothing he loves doing more than talking to strangers about Jesus. John engages in conversation with all sorts of people and discusses subjects like evolution, world religions, cults – anything or anyone that offers an initial barrier to a relationship with Jesus Christ.

John left his position as manager at a well-known London High Street name to become a train guard. Some might ask why. John says: "I have more time, less stress which means more opportunities to talk to people about Jesus." It seems his train is truly bound for glory!

When people ask John what he does for a living he always tells them but only after explaining "that he talks to people about Jesus". Some would say that John is an evangelist but John is not so sure; he prefers the description witness or seed sower. He says, "I am only doing what Jesus asked his disciples to do, no-more no less.

"When I am going out to speak with people I always feel nervous and apprehensive. I'm aware people are thinking 'Here comes that nutter'. And in a small town like I live in, it is harder than witnessing in London. In the capital I'll probably not see anyone I come across again, but where I live I am a familiar face. They probably think: 'Oh, no it's that religious fanatic.' But I accept that label, it's all a part of being a Christian, or at least it should be!"

John recently paid for 1,500 tracts to be printed so, "There are lots of people that are going to be meeting me in the next year or so!"

John Hughes is doing what he passionately believes God wants him to do. He is certain and challenges all disciples of Jesus to "get out there and start proclaiming the Good News".

He is not a well-known Christian: he doesn't appear on Christian TV, he doesn't write books and he is not a famous evangelist or preacher, but he is faithfully obeying Jesus Christ by doing God's will. In John, Jesus has a real "doer" for the kingdom.

Just think of the thousands of other unsung Christian heroes that the world has never heard of, like John. The world thinks they are just "weirdos" or worse! But to Jesus, the one everyone has to give an account of their lives to, they are his trusted and faithful servants. Let's ask ourselves: who do we want to be like, the spiritually lazy or the kingdom doer?

◤ Try this!

Here is a challenge for you. Make two lists, and in the first one write down all the names of people who do tasks for you on a regular basis. Next to their name write down the type of task they carry out for you.

For the second list, put down the names of the people for whom you carry out tasks. Again, next to each name, write down the type of task you do for each of them.

Then compare each list. What do you find? Is one list longer than the other? Does this exercise show that you are doing more for others, or are others doing more for you? How does this challenge you?

Remember, the point of this exercise is not to see how good we are helping others, nor is to make ourselves feel bad about what we are not doing, but it is a practical way to have a good look at ourselves and to see whether we can do more for others than we are doing already.

For "doing" it is always important to have the right attitude; that goes for whether we are praying, giving or going – we must be genuine. The right attitude means we won't be compelled to do the right thing but we will do the right thing because we want to. We have already determined that if our hearts are not sincere and right before God then we will be in for troubled times. The principle applies to doing. As always the subject is covered in the Bible, so let's consider what it says about our attitude as disciples and what doing should not be. We'll read it from *The Message* translation:

The world is not a stage (Matthew 6:2–4; *The Message*)

"When you do something for someone else, don't call attention to yourself. You've seen them in action, I'm sure – 'playactors' I call them – treating prayer and street corner alike, as a stage, acting compassionate as long as someone is watching, playing to the crowds. They get applause, true, but that's all they get. When you help someone out, don't think about how it looks. Just do it – quietly and unobtrusively. That is the way your God, who conceived you in love, working behind the scenes, helps you out."

Jesus Christ is not a mindset

You and I live in a world that by most accounts has given up on truth. Intellectual men

In our doing, we need to develop good habits, especially in our relationship with God. Here are six "habits" that I am developing in my life, and daily trying to live out to the best of my ability. I have listed them below using the first letter in the word "habits" to begin each point:

H: Holding on to time with God – praying and listening.

A: Accountability with another believer.

B: Bible memorization and living it out.

I: Involvement in the Body of Christ, as well as in the youth group.

T: Tithing in time and in money.

S: Study of the Scriptures, digging deep below the pages

and women in their ivory towers get together and have brainstorming sessions. They come to conclusions like, "We have reasoned by philosophical, psychological and sociological disciplines that there is no such thing as absolute truth, so no one can say they know complete truth." And many of the world's people think, "Wow, that's really heavy, it must be true." But how can it be true if the men and women with the big brains say that there is no such thing as truth? If they are right, why should we believe them?

After all how can we know what they say is true if there is no such thing as complete truth?

You see, the world's cleverest cannot give truly sensible answers to the deep yearnings of the human heart. A lot of their ideas change, they are subjective (personal opinion) and based on the limits of their brains. What they attempt to do is convert you to a mindset but it doesn't seem to matter which one – "Pick and choose", they say. "There's plenty to go around. As long as you are happy that's the main thing."

This is when Jesus Christ towers like the God he is over the concept and thought patterns of man. Let's just compare their conclusions to what we know when we choose to follow Jesus. The world's ideas change: God never changes. The world says allow for subjectivity: God is omniscient (all-knowing), he doesn't have opinions – the truth is his objective. The world says choose what suits you, there are many ways: Jesus says he is the only way.

When people argue about their views they are trying to win someone over to their way of thinking. Now, some Christians when they are defending the Faith sadly get into this thought wave but Jesus is not an alternative; he is not a mind "ology" or a good idea. He is not an argument winner. He is quite simply the TRUTH. He is the Word of God (that can only be truthful) made flesh. He is the living, breathing, walking TRUTH. He is the "being" of TRUTH.

As Jesus' disciples we are supposed to be "beings" of TRUTH. Okay, until Heaven and our new bodies that God promises us, we are stained by sin still but because of the Holy Spirit we can resist sin. Put it this way: if we are his disciples then we certainly shouldn't be sinning as much as we once did!

You see there isn't a starting point with Jesus like there is with "ology" subjects. Jesus didn't suddenly appear on Christmas Eve as a baby: he pre-existed his human life! Meaning, like his Father and the Holy Spirit, Jesus has always existed. Mind blowing, amazing, awesome, scary and there are hundreds of other adjectives we use to describe his majesty but the fact remains in him is the TRUTH.

If someone says that is a lie, then they are wrong. I'm not trying to be flippant or arrogant but you see, the non-believer in Jesus Christ is blind to the TRUTH. Firstly the non-believer is a created being, God isn't. God created the non-believer. The clever men and women who come up with brain power statements like "There is no such thing as truth", or "We are only a little higher than apes" (monkeys that got lucky!) do not realize that it was God who not only created clever humans but also created THOUGHT! Without it they wouldn't function, let alone think their deep and heavy thoughts. A pity really because God doesn't think much of what they think.

1 Corinthians 1:18 "For the message of the cross is foolishness to those who are perishing, but to us who are being saved it is the power of God."

1 Corinthians 1:20–21 "Where is the wise man? Where is the scholar? Where is the philosopher of this age? Has not God made foolish the wisdom of the world? For since in the wisdom of God the world through its wisdom did not know him, God was pleased through the foolishness of what was preached to save those who believe."

Is your heart beating to Jesus' beat?

Sometimes brainpower is important in the building of God's Kingdom – praise God for the clever people he uses to bring his plans to fruition. The majority of us are not geniuses but there is no such thing or excuse for a Jesus disciple not possessing a DOER'S heart.

Christian organizations around the world work incredibly hard, mobilizing people to use their various gifts, in order to serve others in many radical ways. They know that God causes disciples to work out what they believe by DOING. At *What4* we believe that God WORKS. We know, like the thousands of Christians down the ages, that when you know God, you want to do things for him and for others; it's all about being DOERS.

The Bible is quite specific when it comes to encouraging us to get out there and get on with doing our bit. Time after time we are commanded (note – it's not a suggestion or a helpful hint!) to put what we say we believe into practice and do something about it. God says through James (2:17): "Isn't it obvious that God-talk without God-acts is outrageous nonsense?" (*The Message*).

God wants us to be people of action. When you're young you've got energy, enthusiasm and vision. You know that you can change the world, and you're dead keen to get out there and do it. Guess what? That's exactly what God wants you to do!

So where do you start? Well, you need to know what specific things God wants you to do and how he wants you to live. And to do that you need to listen to him. How? Spend time with him, praying, reading what he has written down for you in the Bible; talking to Christians you respect and asking their advice. God will give you a job to do and the skills required, if you're serious! Then go for it. Don't let people or circumstances put you off doing what God has told you to do. And remember: you're not your own. You're part of God's vast army of people throughout the world who are all serving him where he has put them.

"So don't sit around on your hands! No more dragging your feet!" (Hebrews 12:12; *The Message*).

And go for it!

DID YOU KNOW THAT YOUR ACTIONS SPEAK LOUDER THAN WORDS? OUR ACTIONS REFLECT OUR LIFESTYLE AND THIS CAN HAVE AN IMPACT ON OUR PRAYERS TO GOD.

▓ Lifestyle matters

James 5:16–18 talks to us quite clearly that the prayer of a righteous man is powerful. Our lifestyle really counts. God will move when a person honours him by the way that they live – the right lifestyle mean your prayers will be powerful. Words are easy, the world will only know you are genuine when they see what you believe applied to your actions – the way you live should back up what flows from your mouth.

Nightmare Island
By Marco Palmer

The island I want to write about is the opposite of Fantasy Island. It is an island where your worst nightmares could come true. It is an island twelve miles off the Ugandan coast in Lake Victoria. The island is Buvvma. The people live in dire poverty. There are no roads, no hospitals. It is a living nightmare.

Enter two heroes: Shadrak – if that name rings a bell, it is because of the famous Bible story of the three men who were thrown into the flaming furnace as told in the book of Daniel. Our Shadrak is from Uganda. He was able to go to China as a medical student, where he learnt to speak the language and married a Chinese girl. Shadrak is also an "on fire" Christian; so while he was in China it was not surprising that he started three underground churches!

Shadrak has a medical clinic in Uganda's capital, Kampala. He wanted to do something for the suffering people of Buvvma. Shadrak was flown out to the island where its inhabitants had never seen an aeroplane so close before and were amazed that it could even float on the lake.

Shadrak worked day and night for several years and treated 350 patients. He saved the life of a woman who was having a miscarriage. He also met two people dying of Aids and was able to pray for them. They became Christians just two days before they went to be with Jesus. His "doing" really did make a difference!

Our second hero is Phillip Knight of World Gospel Mission. Phillip is doing all kinds of things on Buvvma Island to tackle the horrors that many face. He is bringing medicine, schooling and agricultural projects to Buvvma. The people of Buvvma have a hunger to know God and the message of Jesus and now there are churches beginning to start up on this island.

The fact that people can have their basic needs met is no longer a fantasy. Because of missionaries like Shadrak and Phillip it is a reality.

Mission should encompass our very beings; in all that we do or aspire to do, it should all be done for God and his coming Kingdom. After all it is our true home. Remember God's will *will* be done, but he wants us to be willing to do it.

Wow, just think of all the people who have been helped and led to Jesus because Christians decided to "do" – what life changes occur when we become "doing disciples".

Think about this. If we all chose not to get

up tomorrow, not to do anything for anyone, then everything would grind to a halt – apart from the world turning on its axis, planet earth would come to a standstill. Complete gridlock.

There would be no transport or public services, no heating or lighting, no food to buy, no one to talk to, no one to help if we're in trouble. It would be chaos. It would be the Devil's most wonderful dream come true!

In these desperate conditions we would soon realize how vital it is for us to have all kinds of people doing all kinds of things – a lot of which we simply take for granted especially in the West. Doing is a necessity of life. It might seem obvious to say if we decide not to do, then things will not be done, but it's true.

Okay, the above depressive thought applies to the world. Yes, that's right but equally it applies to our own walks as disciples of Jesus. If his followers become apathetic then the doing will not be done. And just think how ashamed we will be when we are standing in front of Jesus in Heaven and he shows us the thousands upon thousands of people who were never told the Gospel because of our decision on earth not to do anything with the message and gifts that he gave us. And what about when he shows us all those suffering people of the world whom we could have helped improve their lives, had we decided to do something when we had the opportunity. Imagine the guilt when we realize we haven't done what he asked us to do. He then shows us a contrast of all the thousands upon thousands of smiling, joyful men, women and children who are so happy because of the Christians of generations past who did do what God asked them to do for the lost of their lifetime.

Feeling totally downhearted? Good, so you should. But cheer up because that is only a depiction of what may happen if we choose not to do the things that he is asking of us. But what amazing blessings we will receive if we decide to get out there and become "doers" for God! We can truly change the world. There are so many opportunities for us to grab hold of. Not doing is not an option, there are too many lost people waiting to be rescued from their personal hell on earth and the Hell of eternity.

The incredible fact is that God has chosen us fallen humans to help him. He has done everything possible to give us the keys to his Kingdom; he has paved the way. When Jesus died on the cross at Calvary he did something completely ungraspable. He bridged the chasm (massive gap) between sinful man and God the Father. By human standards death on a cross is a cruel way to die but throughout history many people have suffered death in order to set others free. Yet what Jesus did was utterly staggering.

He gave up paradise to become a man and live among sinners. Now let's face it, we understand that sin is bad and we can see its consequences. One only has to look at the divorce rate, adultery, lies, murder, abortion, hate, hurt, envy, lack of respect, stealing, mugging, greed… And so and so on. But because we have a sinful nature we become desensitized to sin's effects on our corrupted flesh. But to God sin is total abomination. So do you see from Jesus' point of view what he was entering when he became a baby almost 2,000 years ago?

Even though Jesus never sinned he had to spend time with people who did on a moment-by-moment basis; people who did not care for him, even hated the sight of him. We will never know what the perfect God/man had to endure when he walked amongst us and when he sacrificed his life after sickening torture and humiliating suffering for all who would come to him. And remember that physically it was a terrible way to die. But Jesus died at the hands of the ones he had created. Just try and understand what that must have been like to hang naked for all to see and be mocked by the people you had come to save from themselves and an eternity separated from all goodness, where God's light will never shine. Perhaps the most gut-wrenching injustice was the fact he had done nothing wrong. He died in innocence to set the guilty free.

Be assured of this wonderful fact: in Jesus Christ we have the perfect example of how we are to live our lives by doing the will of the Father.

Jesus had to make a decision to "set his face like flint" towards Jerusalem and towards his own death. Some decisions to "do" are not taken lightly. The cost might mean a great sacrifice. But for believers to sacrifice something or ourselves for the right reasons will be a person's gain in Heaven: the rewards will far exceed the costs.

As Jesus prayed in the Garden of Gethsemane (Luke 22:42): "Not my will, but yours be done", so we too must allow God's will to be first in our lives. Jesus' decision was not easy for him to bear, and for a while he wrestled with his fears of what was to come – the crucifixion! "Father, if you are willing, take this cup from me." But he came to the place within himself where he understood that his will had to be surrendered to allow God's will to be carried out. "Not my will, but yours be done." This account is a wonderful reminder of the humanity of Jesus and the victory that Christ secured over his fears. This account also shows that he, too, in sharing in our fears and struggles understands those very same fears within each one of us.

By now we must realize that doing can really cost, but if our doing is for God then it will always be worth it.

So where should we start doing? Well, the answer is quite simple, but the outworking is a little more complicated. This is because we all need to start in our own "Jerusalem", the place where we find ourselves in right now. Think about it: if we can't share Jesus where we live, work and meet up with our friends, then it would be like living a double standard if we began sharing Jesus in places where nobody knew us.

To finish let's look at what Jesus said should be our overriding focus when considering our motives in everything we do. Read Matthew 22:34–40. It's no surprise that to love God with all our heart, soul and mind, should be our central mindset. But then out of this we are encouraged to love our neighbours as ourselves. When this becomes our driving force, then our doing will be generated by a heart that desires to see our neighbours built up, through the love God has graciously given us.

Time for a recap

1. We should "do" because "his" will be done.
2. Because someone decided to do for you what was done for them.
3. Doing means we can practically apply ourselves.
4. You can't "Walk the Talk" unless you start "doing" first.
5. The world will label you a hypocrite if you are not a "doer" of what you believe.
6. Doing means putting faith into practice.

FINAL THOUGHTS

"Think global act local." This is *What4*'s slogan and by now you will have seen that this is something we passionately believe in. But this doesn't just apply to us in *What4* – this is something that we all should be doing as individuals: being global Christians and working this out locally, by praying, giving, going and doing. Isn't it amazing to know that our God is such a limitless God, but chooses to use us, people like you and me!

Here in *What4* we help to play a small part in this gigantic global plan that God is engineering. You too have a role to play. You really do. Don't let anyone rob you of this God-given reality. All true disciples know that action speaks louder than words and that it's not enough only to speak about the things that God is doing but to put these things into practice. In this same way, it is also my hope that in writing down some of the stories and accounts from the ministries of *What4* and of others, you too will be inspired to put into practice what God has given you to do.

If you're still asking: "How do I find the strength/direction to do God's will?" Then take my advice – start by looking at what God says in his Word. A great place to find encouragement and guidance is Acts 1:8:

"But you will receive power when the Holy Spirit comes on you." The Greek word used for "power" here is "Dunamis", where the word "dynamite" is derived from. God knows that we need this awesome power working in and through our lives, before we can be effective in building the kingdom. So we need to first be filled with the Holy Spirit, the third person in the Holy Trinity. Jesus gave direct instructions to his disciples not to leave Jerusalem until they had received "the gift" his Father had promised. The gift Jesus was speaking about was the Holy Spirit, given by God the Father, and Jesus knew how important it was for the disciples to receive this gift and to know God's power in their witness and lives.

Today, the Holy Spirit is available to every believer, and that includes you and me! If you feel powerless, or fearful to step out for God – ask God to give you the Holy Spirit for power and for boldness in your witness, and believe that he will do just that.

"Where should I start? I'm not sure what I have to give to God?"

"Jerusalem": Start where you live, with what you have. Be faithful with what has been given to you already. We all have talents, skills and gifts. Ask God to show you how to make use of these. Then use them within your home, school, church or wherever you are.

"Judea and Samaria": In the time of the first disciples, Judea and Samaria were local districts of Jerusalem and it was important for these disciples to share about Jesus to their neighbours in Jerusalem. The "model" for us is just the same, in that we need to be sharing our faith in our local district and with our neighbours.

"To the ends of the earth": We need to recognize that God has a global plan and that our understanding of evangelism and mission needs to incorporate a willingness to support God's work worldwide.

In the box opposite are some ways in which you can get more information to help you pray, give, go and do.

If anyone is still suffering from spiritual lethargy and you are in need of a wake-up call then just think of all the giants of faith that have gone before you. Jesus, the disciples and the apostles, John the Baptist, Abraham, Moses, Joshua, Daniel, David, Isaiah, and all the other God-believing people in the Old and New Testaments. Then there are the faithful well-known servants outside of the Bible: John Bunyan, William

Local Church: Get involved in a mission-minded church.

Text: A friend who is already "praying, giving, going, doing".

Websites/E-mails: Log-on to websites of mission agencies, both here in the UK and overseas. E-mail them about your interest in getting involved.

Phone: Speak to a contact in these agencies.

Snail-mail: Write a letter and let them know of your interest.

In person: Go and make visits to agencies/organizations; attend conferences and get involved in overseas short- and long-term projects.

Wilberforce, Charles Spurgeon, Martin Luther King and the millions of faithful disciples of their respective generations whose names we don't know but which are sung in Heaven.

Thousands of pages would be filled if we listed all the names of Jesus' true followers – time and space do not allow us that privilege, but let us be lifted up by the fact that they were doers for their time. They did what we are now doing, and in the future and until Jesus returns, others will do what we have done – praise God!

So as we draw to the end of this book, I pray that many of you will be encouraged to be the disciples that God always wanted you to be, and now will do all you can to seek and carry out God's call on your life.

Perhaps there are those of you who will still be asking the question: "When is the right time to share my faith in Jesus?" NOW! is the simplest answer. We started this book exploring the meaning of "discipleship" and it seems right that we should end on this same theme.

It has been a privilege sharing my thoughts and passion with you. Remember that our daily lives need to "shine Jesus", and we need to light the paths of the people we live and work with, the ones who know us best.

All that remains to be said is "get out there" and be a 21st-century disciple of Christ. Do not be afraid. Focus on Jesus. Keep telling yourself that Heaven is real. Jesus is building a place far beyond our imagination, where he will reward his faithful workers and invite them to join him in a new lifetime where wonders, purpose and eternity await.

All the problems, stresses and troubles that we may have suffered on planet earth will pale into insignificance. If we have put our trust in the King of kings then our destiny is assured and what a future – living forever in an amazing new body in paradise will be just the start! All he asks of us is to follow only him and to seek his will at all times. We can only be effective disciples and fishers of men, women and children if we seek and obey and we can only do this if we pray, give, go and do!

Ideas and Resources

SO YOU REALLY WANT TO BE SERIOUS ABOUT JESUS? WELL CHECK OUT THE INFO BELOW

PRAYING

What4's prayer projects: "Powerhouse"

Within *What4* we have set up three prayer projects to help young people pray:

Powerhouse Cells/Links

Forming a Powerhouse Cell means committing time to pray with at least one other person (but as many as you like) on a regular basis about global mission, and about your own needs and issues. *What4* will provide regular prayer updates from various missions, and will also provide you with a prayer diary, so that you can keep track of the things you pray for and record how God answers your prayers!

When we are aware that there are a number of Powerhouse Cells meeting in one area, we encourage them occasionally to meet together to pray in a larger group – this is called a Powerhouse Link. Meeting with other cells can provide a great opportunity to share ideas about prayer, share prayer requests, and generally encourage each other.

Powerhouse update

If you don't feel able to form a cell, but wish to be involved in praying on your own for the work of *What4* and global mission, then why not sign up just to receive the prayer update? Each month we will send you a list of prayer requests, and information about how previous prayer requests have been answered.

Powersurge

Powersurge is *What4*'s mega-prayer event. Each year, we invite young people from all over the UK to come together to pray for the nation. Events take place in the capital cities of each region of the UK – Belfast, Cardiff, Edinburgh and London. The events are led by *What4* team members, and young people are able to pray in the centres of power in each city, such as parliament buildings and law courts. There are opportunities to meet with influential men and women in government and other areas of leadership across the nation. We also link up with other young people from different nations to pray together.

What4 takes prayer very seriously, and rightly so. Where would we be without our communication line to our heavenly Father? He knows what we need, and he wants us to ask him for help. Our relationship with God depends on prayer. So go on, get stuck in and see where God will take you in prayer today!

GIVING

What4 knows that giving is about the attitude of the heart, so whether a person is giving their time, energy or money, it is the heart that must be the driving force. All the projects and outreaches that *What4* is involved in would not get off the ground if people didn't "give". To reach out we need to reach deep within – our hearts as well as our pockets – but when we start giving we receive so much more. God gives when we are willing to give.

GOING

What4 works in partnership with a number of organizations, and it has been a real privilege to see hundreds of young people going and making a difference in the world, as well as mission making a difference in their world!

Some of these overseas projects are one-year missions, working with Christian organizations in developing countries. We have also seen hundreds of young people go on short-term missions, for three to four weeks. It does not matter about the length, it matters about the attitude, and it matters about what you put in! Without exception everyone whom *What4* has helped and enabled to get overseas has come back a totally different person. Their outlook has changed. They see their world differently.

⊚ *What4* overseas teams

What4 sends teams on practical aid and mission projects to some of the poorest areas of the world. These teams are made up of young people who are 16+, working alongside experienced leaders who know what overseas mission is all about. **What4** has been running teams since 1995, and has helped loads of young people to be fired up to serve God.

So what happens on one of these overseas missions? Well, we aim to show God's love to the local people through practical caring action. Each project is geared to the specific needs of the local community. In the past this has involved building clinics, classrooms, reading and literacy centres, vocational training facilities, even airstrips so that MAF planes can land in remoter places! Teams are involved in culturally sensitive missions, supporting the work of the local churches and other mission organisations, for example: setting up children's street clubs, which include health education and basic medical care, alongside games, music, drama, Bible stories and other activities.

When you get back, *What4* will help you to put some of the things you have learned overseas into practice where you live. Ongoing support will be provided, as settling back into your local culture after a cross-cultural mission can be a traumatic experience! *What4* will be on hand to get you through.

DOING

How do you do?

(How you can be a "doer" with *What4*!)

By:

- Becoming a Networker.

- Fundraising for *What4* and related projects.

- Joining *What4*'s GAP Year Programme (Motiv8 year-out scheme).

- Sharing in evangelism teams with *What4*.

What4 Networker scheme

Networkers are young people between the ages of 14 and 21, who want to grow in their Christian faith. They want to learn more about God and to get involved in mission in their local church set-up. They also want to serve God in the work of global mission, and they choose to do this through *What4*.

Networkers are young people who are not afraid to get their hands dirty. They get involved in sharing their Christian faith and inspiring other young people in schools, colleges, youth groups and events. They learn to communicate the Christian message in their local area, and also have opportunities to work with local and national *What4* staff and team members in projects and events further afield throughout the UK.

Neworkers are made up of a team of young people all over the UK who, with the endorsement of their parents/guardians, and their local church, actively support *What4* and the work of other mission organizations through various activities. These include our prayer initiative – Powerhouse, school work just got too much to deal with as well as organizing Christian events within the school. Whilst at school, a lot of us felt that God wanted to do something very powerful there. By the time I left, not much appeared to have changed, and I felt pretty disheartened. But I knew strongly that God still hadn't finished and that he still wanted to use me there, as well as many others. By this stage I felt I had a real 'heart' for young people, in that God was really making me care about them – particularly in my local area of Hythe – and I wanted to continue to put that compassion into action. I had seen the *What4* schools team doing their stuff in my own school and it became clear that God wanted me to be part of that. I prayed about it before deciding, and everything seemed to fall into place, so I joined the team!

"During the year I had some good times, but also some very low moments. I know that's because I was doing what God wanted me to do and Satan didn't like it. I reached the doubting stage many times but my doubts faded because God provided the most incredible opportunities for me to share my own faith in him – now I'm just really excited about what's to come. When I feel weak it's good because I know God will be doing the work, not me, and that's always a good thing!"

"E" for Evangelism:

Another area where *What4* involves young people is in its evangelism programme.

"E" stands for evangelism, and *What4* conducts a programme that will involve you in being trained and equipped in this essential and necessary role. *What4* will help you to share your faith using whatever skills you have. This could be in preaching, but it could just as easily be sharing your "worldly goods", or simply living out your Christian life in front of your friends.

We encourage all those who want to take part in being trained in evangelism to do so through our Networker Team, where one-to-one participation can be encouraged. In turn, *What4* will resource and provide opportunities for those within the Networker team to take part in evangelism in a number of different and challenging settings.

I hope you see the amazing opportunities that God has provided for young people through the ministry of *What4*. We look forward to hearing from you!

To find out more about *What4*, have a look on our website **www.what4.org.uk** or e-mail: janet@what4.org.uk (overseas enquiries) or dave@what4.org.uk (year-out enquiries).